Lantern

Traces of an American Family

For Bill Lass,

Bill M[...]

UNIVERSITY OF IOWA PRESS ᴪ Iowa City

University of Iowa Press,
Iowa City 52242
Copyright © 1997 by
the University of Iowa Press
All rights reserved
Printed in the United States of America

Design by Richard Hendel

http://www.uiowa.edu/~uipress

Printed on acid-free paper

Library of Congress
Cataloging-in-Publication Data
Morgan, William Towner.
    Salt lantern: traces of an American
family / by William Towner Morgan.
        p.   cm.—(The American land and
life series)
    Includes bibliographical references
(p.   ) and index.
    ISBN 0-87745-613-5,
ISBN 0-87745-614-3 (paper)
    1. Morgan, William Towner—Family.
2. Pipestone County (Minn.)—
Biography.   3. Goodhue County
(Minn.)—Biography.   4. North
Dakota—Biography.   5. Holliday
family.   6. Brown family.   7. Morgan
family.   8. Stannard family.
9. Vernacular architecture—
Minnesota—Pipestone County.
I. Title.   II. Series.
CT275.M624A3   1997
977.6′1405′0922—dc21
[B]   97-17333

97 98 99 00 01 02 C
5   4   3   2   1
97 98 99 00 01 02 P
5   4   3   2   1

Salt Lantern

The American Land & Life Series

Edited by Wayne Franklin

Salt

William Towner Morgan

For my aunt

Annie Belle Brown Winters

(1883–1971)

my sister

Courtenay Morgan-Forman

and my niece

Diane Paterson

CONTENTS

Foreword by Wayne Franklin, ix

Prologue, xiii

Acknowledgments, xix

Introduction, xxi

1 The Spaces and Places of My Childhood, 1

2 My Journey to Field Head, England, 22

3 My Journey to Ecclefechan, Scotland, 29

4 The Hallidays' Journey to America, 36

5 My Journey to Checkerberry Village, Vermont, 42

6 The Wisconsin Experience and the Landscape of War, 50

7 The Stannards of Taylors Falls, Minnesota, 57

8 The Hallidays, Hollidays, and Browns of
   Goodhue County, Minnesota, 63

9 The Browns of Pipestone County, Minnesota, 69

10 North Dakota Pioneers: The Hallidays, Hollidays, and Stramblads, 81

11 My Journey to Glencolumbkille, Ireland, 94

12 My Father's Story, 103

Conclusion and Family Album, 115

Appendix 1. "Weighed in the Balance," 131

Appendix 2. The Architecture of a Craftsman Bungalow, 136

Appendix 3. Gen. George J. Stannard, Forgotten Hero
   of the Civil War, 138

Appendix 4. "Fifteen Months on a North Dakota Claim," 143

Notes, 153

Index, 171

Even when we are not conspicuously rooted, bedded in the earth the way our agricultural ancestors were, our lives *take place*. We are likely to use that expression offhandedly, without really noticing how it reveals the ties that bind our experience to the earth beneath us, around us, indeed even in us. Much of modern history has been a flight from the consequences of our dependence on the land, with the added irony that the ways by which we seek to hide that fact — fossil fuels, for instance — not only derive from the earth but also, in our abuse of them, rebound on it and ultimately on us. We take as freedom from gravity what is only the decreasing velocity of a failed escape into the stratosphere of illusion. If only because we shall come back down again, we should be careful what we jettison as we rise.

Our memories, another kind of gravity, often are so colored with the details of place that even in an age of postmodern dislocations we are haunted by the afterimage of old locales. We ought to attend to such memories, for they tell us a great deal about ourselves and our situation on earth. We require liberation not from the earth, for all our culture seems aimed at that vain wish; we require liberation instead from the notion that this is just another planet around another star, as if any other — or none at all — would suit us just as well. We need most of all a sense of the precious, the actual, what Alfred North Whitehead called the *value* of things. The earth is incommensurably our own, not as possession but as setting, the concrete actual scene of our lives. We are members of it; we take place here.

Books often accelerate toward an escape of their own, shielding us from the terms of our life here, but books at their best also can remind us of the necessary earth. This is particularly true, I think, of memoirs, and

William Towner Morgan's is a good example. Morgan's title for the book, *Salt Lantern*, captures nicely the spirit of his narrative. Seemingly mysterious although composed of two common, even ordinary elements, the title suggests by the wonder of its own chemistry the transformative power in the odd conjunctions of every life. Morgan floats the ordinary details of one life on the sea of memories — passed on in family stories, photographs, and artifacts — that have given it shape and meaning. He is especially good at evoking from the most unforthcoming item, like the salt lantern itself, whole realms of significance. He shows the past not as a collection of forgotten items stuffed into some box in the universal attic of our lives but rather as a fertile field full of footprints, traces, clues. All we lack, he makes us understand, is a talent for seeing what we seek. Luck in uncovering where we come from is two-thirds patience.

The impulse to solve that puzzle is broadly human, but it is one in which Americans have been well schooled by experience. Whether our ancestors came here in slave ships or on the *Mayflower*, landed first among the French at Biloxi in 1710 or the Bohemians at Ellis Island in 1910, or indeed were here already when the first of the outsiders arrived, we all share a sense of uprooting, of the shifting scene of our identities and lives, that makes us curious to untangle the knotted strands of memory by going backward in time. We have, most of us, a few narrative bits, odd photos, objects (without stories, often enough), threaded on a yearning for a more complete tale. Morgan had much of this, along with a sense of belatedness (which I'll let him explain) that gave the broad American impulse a peculiar personal poignancy for him.

He has had extraordinary success in finding and reading the traces. In a narrative that spans the ocean and links together five branches of his family past, he localizes with piquant detail the habits, as well as habitations, of a rich cast of characters. At Field Head farm in Cumbria, England, and the impressive dwelling his American relatives dubbed the "salt lantern house," located near Field Head in the village of Great Strickland, his explorations in his family's past produced surprisingly intact results. His tale of how he found the latter place, its image long burned into his mind through the sketch of it inserted in that lantern, reads like a modern odyssey. The first part of it was conducted in a taxicab, but thereafter an ice storm forced him to go ahead on foot, so the effort was properly reduced to the terms laid down by Nature.

Through other stretches of his odyssey, Morgan found houses or house sites scattered in Ireland, Vermont, North Dakota, Texas, as well as his own birth region of the upper Midwest. The dwellings he found or recalled include the large, stylish Craftsman "semibungalow" built by his parents in Pipestone, Minnesota, in 1919; the Victorian residence of his maternal grandparents next door; the farms in Tiffany, Wisconsin, and Florence, Minnesota, where his great-grandparents settled after leaving the Great Strickland house and migrating to North America in 1855; and a claim shack and several pioneer farmhouses on the Dakota prairie where another branch settled. Morgan sought out these places with patience, and he saw them with the precision of a sometime field surveyor for the Historic American Buildings Survey, but they do not appear in the story merely for the sake of their crisp details. Throughout his travels, Morgan's interest lay in pattern and meaning. When he had located and visited enough of the old family sites, it thus occurred to him that the various members of various branches of his family tended to settle down on landscapes uncannily similar to each other, whether in England or North Dakota. It is as if these places carried forward to him in their multiple echoes some finer trace of memory, something no mere collection of details could provide. Everywhere, Morgan managed to dig around in the physical and social environment sufficiently to unearth other, similar insights.

However they may be constituted, however unfamiliar they may be to us in practice, we all have families. For that reason, I suppose we ought to take some sympathetic interest in the families of others, but we rarely do, too often overhearing in genealogical investigations a kind of private conversation. William Towner Morgan's story is only incidentally, though, about his own forebears. It more pertinently speaks to all of us, describing a search we long to make, an effort to locate ourselves in the landscapes of this actual world. Unlike most of us, Morgan had the will to begin and the grit to finish. He consequently gives to all of us a metaphor for how we also fit in, how we, too, belong to the surfaces of this extraordinary planet. As it is lighted in the prose of his fine memoir, the lantern that has served as a peculiar icon of his family's journey illuminates the world at large.

PROLOGUE

When I was a child growing up in Pipestone, Minnesota, my aunt Anne and uncle George Winters lived next door in the house my grandfather Warrington Brown built at the turn of the century. When my mother sent me there on errands, I would ask my aunt to open her china cabinet so I could see Great-Grandmother Anne Kilner Halliday's salt-filled chimney lantern.

If I begged her long enough, my aunt would place the lantern on the dining room table so I could gaze at the drawing of the house pressed against the lantern's glass surface. As I marveled over its strange imagery, I must have wondered about the lantern's significance, especially the picture of the house. The memory of the salt lantern has stayed with me all my life.

The salt lantern is a globe from a kerosene lamp filled with sea salt and personal mementos that commemorate my great-grandmother's English home and her journey to America in 1855. On one side is an ink drawing of a house framed with wintergreen leaves and cloth flowers that may have come from Great-Grandmother Halliday's wedding dress. On the lantern's reverse side are images of the British lion and the unicorn, an American eagle, several native English plants, and a sundial.

When I was older, Aunt Anne told me there was a real "salt lantern house" in the English village of Great Strickland, in Westmorland (now Cumbria) County, and that John and Anne Kilner Halliday had lived in that house for two years before coming to America. Anne Kilner was born in 1824 at Field Head, a farm near Great Strickland. Her father, John Kilner, built the salt lantern house as a wedding gift.

The salt lantern stood in my grandmother Brown's china cabinet for over seventy years. The beautifully executed drawing was done by Samuel Reynolds, a London schoolmaster, who boarded with John and Anne Halliday in the salt lantern house.

THE QUEEN'S OWN.

Pictures of the lion and the unicorn, an American eagle, native English amaranthus plants, and a sundial appear on the lantern's reverse side. The plants are grown in England, where they symbolize constancy, fidelity, faith, and immortality. This salt lantern, a Victorian artifact, celebrates the ideals of home and family.

As I was growing up, my aunt told me many stories about my English and Scottish ancestors. In 1984, while teaching in England, I visited Field Head, and four years later I returned to the village to try to find the salt lantern house. On a frosty February morning, I took a taxi to Great Strickland from Penrith, where I had been staying. After leaving the main highway, the taxi hit ice on the country road that wound into the village. When the driver said he feared he might slide off the hilly road if he continued farther, I agreed to complete my journey on foot. After walking about a mile in the brisk winter air, I came upon a house at the town's west end with the three chimneys I remembered from the picture in the salt lantern. Unchanged from the day the artist drew it was my great-grandparents' salt lantern house.

John Kilner built the limestone house our family calls the salt lantern house for his daughter Anne and son-in-law John Halliday. Relatively unchanged since the 1850s, the building has been used as a home, a school, and a youth center. In 1997 Marjorie Vaux purchased the house; she is in the process of restoring it to its original use.

ACKNOWLEDGMENTS

I am indebted to several people who have supported my work over the years. My St. Cloud State University colleagues, Arthur Mehrhoff, Pamela Mittlefehldt, Kent Robertson, Eleanore Stokes, and Lewis Wixon, encouraged my work from the outset. David Rambow and his staff at the Pipestone County (Minnesota) Historical Society extended their time and services to me for over a decade. Marilyn Nelson has been a patient assistant throughout the writing of this work.

I am also indebted to the descendants of the Halliday and Brown families, including Ellen and Robert Holliday, Florence Jean Holliday Foster, Dorothy Haltom, and Millicent Remington Owen. My cousin, the late Warrington W. Winters, and his daughter, Anne Winters-Williamson, shared field notes from their journeys to England. David Fallowfield and Dorothy Smith, descendants of the Kilners, accompanied me on my travels in England and Scotland and have continued to be faithful correspondents. Cousin Ihla Donaldson lent me the journal kept by Grandfather Brown during his trip to Boston in 1924 to attend a GAR convention. My collection of family mementos has grown through the generosity of Ihla's gifts.

Current residents who live in my ancestors' homes and who kindly opened their doors to me include George, Eleanor, Julia, and Ian Harrison, Cumbria County, England; John Thomson, George Irving, and Maybell Irving, Ecclefechan, Scotland; and Joe McGinley, Glencolumbkille, County Donegal, Ireland. In my American travels people who offered their assistance include Ivan Sanderson, Milton, Vermont; Harry, Selma, and Martha Stark, Janesville, Wisconsin; Hazel Wimmer and William F. Witt, Lake City, Minnesota; Jane Smith, Steele, North Dakota; Emerson O.

Liessman, Bismarck, North Dakota; and Kaye Grossmann, Taylors Falls, Minnesota.

In many ways this work has been a family project. My deepest gratitude, therefore, goes to my brothers, W. Stannard, George Alan, and Loran (Bud) Morgan, and my sister, Courtenay Morgan-Forman, whose stories and memoirs form part of my narrative. The personal and editorial support of the following brought this work to completion: Diane Paterson, Wayne Franklin, Susan Rugh, Pamela Mittlefehldt, Judy DeVoe, Marilyn Brinkman, and Rosemary Christianson.

INTRODUCTION

In the fall of 1932, my father, William T. Morgan, age forty-nine, cut himself on a barbed wire fence while hunting. The wound refused to heal. As
vice president of Pipestone's First National Bank, my father had agonized
for months about the possibility of bank failure due to the Great Depression. That Christmas, he came down with influenza, and before he had a
chance to recover, he returned to work on New Year's Day. A few days
later, meningitis developed as a result of the untreated wound and a re-
lapse from the flu, and my father slipped into a coma from which he never
recovered.

My father's unexpected death left my pregnant mother, Mabelle Brown
Morgan, forty-five, with four teenage children at home. Three months
later, she gave birth to me. Between the ages of two and four, my constant
companion was my grandfather Warrington Brown. The stories my grandfather told me while we sat on his porch swing are among my earliest and
fondest memories.

When I was four, Grandfather and Grandmother Mary Brown, both in
their early nineties, died. My sister, Courtenay, and my oldest brother,
Stannard, married before I was five, and my other brothers, Alan and
Loran, left home when I was a child to attend the University of Minnesota.
Intermittently, in the 1930s and early 1940s, my brothers acted as surro-
gate fathers, but when they went off to the war, Mother and her sister
Anne took over the duty of raising me.

After my siblings were gone, Mother and I lived alone in the Craftsman
bungalow where I was born. My parents had built the house in 1918 to
shelter their growing family. Next door stood Grandfather Brown's Victorian house, which he had built in 1898 after leaving his farm to start an

implement business. Aunt Anne and Uncle George Winters moved there to care for my grandparents during their declining years, and after their deaths they stayed on in the house the rest of their lives. Some of my most cherished memories were forged within the walls of these two wonderful houses.

It was in my grandparents' house where I first heard the stories about my English great-grandmother Anne Kilner's courtship and marriage to John Halliday, a man whom Anne's father once disparagingly called a "lowly Scot shoemaker." Sitting at my grandparents' dining room table, I was also told that William Kilner, my great-grandmother's brother, lost the family farm, Field Head, in a card game. Other stories were told about how the Brown family survived the blizzards of the 1880s on their prairie claim near Pipestone.

In the spring of 1944, when I was eleven, I spent three restless months in bed recovering from rheumatic fever. To keep me amused during that time, Aunt Anne began writing a memoir that she called "Weighed in the Balance" (appendix 1), the story of the Kilner, Halliday, and Brown families. Over a period of several weeks, my aunt would walk across the lawn that separated our houses to bring me hand-written sections of her work-in-progress. That fall, Aunt Anne took over the duties of caring for two grandchildren when her son and daughter-in-law entered the armed services. "Weighed in the Balance" was set aside and, sadly, never completed.

Aunt Anne was the first person to inspire my development as a family historian. Other people influenced me as well. My mother told me stories about the Hallidays, Browns, and Morgans. Aunt Ruth Donaldson, my mother's youngest sister, also told family stories and challenged my mind with parlor games, crossword puzzles, and quizzes about American history. Until I began my research in 1984, these experiences and stories had been kept in the back of my mind.

At that time, most of our family's diaries, letters, and heirlooms, including the family Bible, had been lost, destroyed, or given away to relatives who were living outside of Minnesota. More importantly, my mother and my aunts had died. Fortunately, some written sources were still available, including the text of "Weighed in the Balance," which throughout the years I had carried from place to place, several family letters and heirlooms, as well as fresh memoirs that I asked my sister and brothers to write as my work progressed. Other documents, including a published excerpt from John Halliday's journal of his voyage to America in 1855 and a travel journal Grandfather Brown kept during a visit to Vermont in 1924, were indispensable to my research.[1]

In the first chapter, I explore my experience growing up in a small town during the Great Depression and World War II. My life at that time was shaped by my close relationship with my mother, my grandfather, and my aunt, by living with older siblings in a single-parent home, and by spending a prolonged period in bed with rheumatic fever. All this experience took place in two homes: 310 and 320 Third Avenue Southwest, Pipestone, Minnesota. The special spirit that resided within the walls of these two houses formed my early interest in family history, material culture, and architecture.

Because most of the stories I had heard as a child were told about my family's maternal side, I began my research by visiting England, where, in the village of Great Strickland, I found the salt lantern house and, nearby, my great-grandmother's farm, Field Head. I then traveled to Ecclefechan, Scotland, where I visited Brownmoor, my great-grandfather John Halliday's farm. A later journey took me to the village of Glencolumbkille, County Donegal, Ireland, the birthplace of my paternal grandmother, Susan Maxwell.

I began my American journey to find the places where the Hallidays and their descendants settled after leaving England in 1855. As I traveled from Vermont to Wisconsin, Minnesota, and North Dakota, I searched for the buildings, landscapes, and stories related to the Hallidays and the family branches that became intertwined through marriage. During the early nineteenth century, two branches, the Browns and Stannards, lived near each other in northwestern Vermont, where my great-grandfather Jason Brown met his future wife, Sarah Stannard. In 1857, Jason and Sarah Brown left Vermont to settle near Sarah's brother, Loammi Stannard, near Janesville, Wisconsin. In 1861, Jason Brown enlisted in the Union army and, during the opening engagement at Bull Run, was killed as his regiment ascended Henry Hill. Three years later, Jason's son, Warrington Brown, age nineteen, received a serious head wound while storming the barricades at Petersburg, Virginia, during the closing engagement of the war.

Following the Civil War, the Brown and Halliday families moved to

Goodhue County, Minnesota, where Warrington Brown and Mary Halliday married and began raising a family. Lured by the virgin prairie farmland of southwestern Minnesota, the Browns moved on to Pipestone County in 1878. In the 1890s, John and Anne Halliday, driven by the pioneer spirit, tried to homestead in North Dakota; when that enterprise failed, they returned to Pipestone to live with their daughter and son-in-law. John and Anne Halliday's son, John Francis Holliday, and a grandchild, Marilla Holliday, also staked claims in central and northwestern North Dakota. Warrington and Mary Brown's life in Goodhue and Pipestone Counties and the experiences of the Hallidays and Hollidays in North Dakota are the subject of my middle chapters.

The story of my Morgan heritage is told in the two final chapters. In 1867, my paternal grandmother, Susan Maxwell, emigrated from Ireland to Illinois and later moved to Story County, Iowa, where she met and married Joseph Homer Morgan, a widowed farmer born in New York State. In 1882, Joseph and Susan Morgan moved to a farm near Pipestone, Minnesota. The final link in my family heritage occurred when Joseph and Susan Morgan's son, William, married Warrington and Mary Brown's daughter, my mother, Mabelle Courtenay Brown Morgan.

I have told my family's story by studying their landscapes and material culture — houses, farm buildings, and a scattering of artifacts. During the course of my research, I found that the Hallidays built their farms in America on or near imposing landscapes, a pattern formed from their memory of home-place landscapes in Scotland and England and repeated as the family settled across the American continent. The westward-moving Yankee pioneers, the Brown and Stannard families, selected a building style (Greek Revival) that reflected their New England heritage.

At each family site, I interviewed current residents to try to understand the changes that took place after my ancestors moved on to other places. I found that the laws and traditions honored in the British Isles often protect buildings and landscapes; therefore, all my ancestors' homes are lived in today (although in Scotland, four concrete nuclear storage silos stand within sight of John Halliday's front door). While these sites have remained relatively intact, immense changes have taken place on American soil. Most of my ancestors' farms from Vermont to North Dakota have been razed in the name of progress. Ironically, in Goodhue County,

Minnesota, John Halliday's farm lies in the path of a proposed nuclear dumpsite.

Several scholarly works have inspired my pursuit of family history, photography, and studies in material culture. Two works that capture the writer's lonely search for family heritage are Catherine Hanf Noren's *Camera of My Family* and Dorothy Redford's *Somerset Homecoming*.[2] My knowledge of vernacular buildings was shaped by my own brief experience with a Historic American Buildings Survey team during the summer of 1978 in Perry, Missouri. I have also been encouraged by the works of Henry Glassie and Howard Wight Marshall.[3] I also owe a special debt to James Deetz, who, during my participation in a 1986 dig at Flowerdew Hundred Plantation in Hopewell, Virginia, taught me how to bring life to mute fragments from the American past.[4]

Wright Morris's photographs taught me to appreciate the beauty of vernacular architecture. Like Morris, I have tried through my photographs, especially those of abandoned sites, to perceive the lives of earlier inhabitants by recording what I feel is the human essence of a landscape, a building, or a ruin. A comment in Morris's preface to *The Inhabitants* helped me to understand how seemingly insignificant material fragments, even those isolated from a human context, can provide insights into family heritage: "apparently I had more than texture in mind on the evidence of the subjects I assembled. Doors and windows, gates, stoops, samples of litter, assorted junk, anything that appeared to have served its purpose. Except people. *Only in their absence will the observer intuit, in full measure, their presence in the subject.*"[5]

The Spaces and Places of My Childhood

Like many babies born during the Great Depression, I was delivered at home. During the delivery, my sister, who had been sent next door to my grandparents' house, could hear my mother's screams. Although I have met others who were born at home, I know of no one else who was delivered by a former veterinarian. (My physician, Alexander Hugh Brown, left veterinary medicine, completed his medical training, and cared for thousands of babies during his long career.)

When my siblings retell the story of my birth, they express a sense of wonder, because our mother had been told that she was too old to bear a child. During her fourth month, a Minneapolis physician informed Mother that she was entering menopause — a woman of forty-six, he argued, simply could not become pregnant. Without further examination, he said that Mother might have a tumor. Several months later, a Sioux Falls physician told Mother, "Go home and get ready for the birth of your baby!"[1]

Three months before my birth, my father had died in the upstairs northeast bedroom. At the time of his death there were four children at home: W. Stannard (Stan), twenty-one; Mary Courtenay (Court), nineteen; George Alan (Alan), seventeen; and Loran Brown (Bud), fourteen. I was born in the middle downstairs bedroom, my mother's bedroom and private retreat. Our hand-wound, floor-model 1913 Edison phonograph once stood in that room. As a child, I would put on my uncle Paul Brown's World War I helmet and march in place while playing "Over There" and "Bing, Bang, Bing 'em on the Rhine." When I think of that room I can smell the machine oil from the inside of the Edison.

My earliest memory is from my creeping stage. When I was eight months old, I struck my head very hard against the sharp end of one of the feet of our large oak rocker. I remember the horrible shock of impact and the sight of the path of blood as I crept from the living room to the sun parlor. It was the first time I remember being *me* and of being alive in a specific place and space. My next recollection is of a scene in the northeast bedroom, the same room where my father had died three years before. Stan is lying on his back on the bed as I sit on his upraised knees. We are playing a game:

> Look at the floor.
> (pause)
> Look at the walls.
> (longer pause)
> SEE THE SPIDER ON THE CEILING!

Just as he speaks the last words, Stan drops me through his knees. I remember anticipating the scary thrill of falling through space.

This kind of sibling bonding was extremely rare after my sister and brothers left home, but Grandfather Brown and I were inseparable friends. While tree frogs sang in the giant elms and cottonwoods that he had planted before the turn of the century, Grandfather and I passed long summer afternoons on the lawn that separated his house and mine. When the noon sun forced us indoors, we retreated to the squeaky swing on the screened porch, where Grandfather promised to take me "up north" on a horse-pulled lumber wagon. To my three-year-old mind, "up north" meant not northern Minnesota but rather the trunk of the huge elm that stood a few feet from the porch steps. I remember sitting absolutely still on the swing, totally absorbed in Grandfather's stories and wondering how a wagon could climb a tree.

Grandfather liked to play "Hide the Thimble" with his grandchildren. During the Civil War, following the death of his father at Bull Run, Grandfather Warrington at age nineteen enlisted in a Wisconsin regiment. A few days short of the war's end, at Petersburg, Virginia, Grandfather was struck at the top of his skull by a minié ball while he and two comrades, both of whom were killed, were charging the barricades at Fort Mahone. Nine days later, a surgeon in Washington, D.C., removed the ball, repaired the wound, and inserted a silver plate at the bottom of the one-inch-deep hole. When I was a child, this hole was quite visible after Grandfather became bald. When Grandfather and I played our game, I knew where he would hide the thimble at least once!

Along with all my nephews, nieces, and cousins, at age five I began taking piano lessons from Aunt Anne Winters. Anne had an ornate, cherry-wood Chickering with chipped-edged and yellowed keys. Her pupils had to sit beside her on the hard bench, precisely in front of middle C, a key that fell beneath the K on the piano's logo. Anne praised us when we rounded our hands properly and gently chastised us when we let them fall on the keyboard. Her own demonstration of a proper arch was accompanied by the sound of her fingernails tapping on the keys. After each lesson, Anne wrote detailed instructions for the coming week's home practice in a red, staff-ruled composition book.

We took our piano lessons in a large, cube-shaped Victorian house that Grandfather had built after he became a prosperous implement dealer. The house was designed to shelter my grandparents and their six children: Paul, Warrington, Garfield, Anne, Mabelle, and Ruth. Grandfather had purchased a large corner lot to provide ample space for a house and his beloved trees — elms and birches on the boulevard, cottonwoods along the alley. For a few brief days in early summer, the cottonwoods produced a blizzard of white, fluffy seeds that lodged in the grass and trees.

I imagine Grandfather chose the Third Avenue (then called South Anna Street) lot because it reminded him of his Vermont childhood home, where houses are built near church, school, and township hall. (In fact, two years after Grandfather built his house, the fine quartzite courthouse was erected within sight of his porch, and the First Presbyterian Church

Five generations of Hallidays, Browns, Winters, and Donaldsons lived at 320 Third Avenue Southwest, Pipestone, Minnesota, from 1898 to 1962. Ruth Brown, twelve, and Mabelle Brown, sixteen, appear in this ca. 1903 photograph.

was built a brisk two-block walk away. By the 1930s, the elegant wrap-around porch had been reduced to a narrow, screened-in bay on the north where Grandfather told his stories from the porch swing and Uncle George napped away lazy summer afternoons.

A person could enter my grandparents' house in one of two ways. The informal way was through the north porch door that opened into a combination sitting and dining room. The formal way of entering was through the front door. This door had a large, translucent center pane of frosted glass surrounded by square panels of stained glass. Below the glass was a brass bell with a raised design and a flange that made a loud, metallic *burrr*. Behind this door was a small vestibule with doors leading to the parlor on the left and the living room on the right. When I carried mail during Christmas vacations from college, the vestibule, with its trapped warm air, made a sunny winter refuge from the cold outdoors.

In my grandparents' day, the parlor where Grandfather and I played "Hide the Thimble" was well lighted, warm, and cozy. Behind the parlor was the tiny bedroom where Grandmother Brown spent her final days. During the decades following my grandparents' deaths, Aunt Anne and

COURT HOUSE

PIPESTONE, MINN. C179

In 1901, Pipestone's jasper quartzite, Renaissance Revival courthouse was completed and the Civil War navy cannon mounted in place. The following year, Leon H. Moore, a talented artist and local businessman, sculpted the Soldiers Monument, on which the names of two hundred veterans of the Civil and Spanish-American Wars appear. When I was a child, I always looked for my grandfather's name. During World War II, the cannon was hauled away for scrap.

Uncle George, now alone, remodeled the rooms downstairs. The north rooms — living, dining, and kitchen — became their living quarters, and the south rooms — parlor, sitting room, and a new kitchen — were later rented to the Heathfield family, who had lost their house when they could no longer make their mortgage payments. My warm-hearted aunt told the family they could rent the south rooms until they could find another place. This arrangement, supposed to last but a few months, turned into a

The First Presbyterian Church was the site of christenings, confirmations, and funerals for the Halliday, Brown, and Morgan families. As a child, lost in reverie, I watched the patterns cast by the sun passing through the stained-glass windows.

thirteen-year occupancy. The saying "When are the Heathfields leaving?" became a family joke that Aunt Anne, Mother, and I shared for years.

When I was a child, my grandparents' basement, upstairs, and attic were special places. The basement is the single exception to my lifelong aversion to below-ground rooms. When I was a boy, I loved the responsibility of stoking the furnace in the warm and pleasant-smelling basement.

To reach the second floor, we children climbed the cherrywood staircase with its railings rubbed raw from years of use. A deeply incised circle design with a small ball in the center was carved into the newel. At the top of the post was a removable ball — one of the places where Grandfather would sometimes hide the thimble. A mixture of dreams and reality marks my memories of the upstairs hallway and bedrooms. In my dreams, a cavernous darkness, tinged with illness and death, surrounds the rooms where my grandparents slept before they became too ill to climb stairs. After Uncle George's death in 1947, the rooms became a storage area. Aunt Anne saved everything. Her tables and desks were piled high with boxes, papers, books, and empty medicine bottles. Unused furniture and bric-a-brac found their way into the second-floor bedrooms. When I was in high school, Mother and Aunt Anne read newspaper accounts of the eccentric brothers who died leaving a mansion in Harlem filled with years of accumulated goods. The name and habits of these brothers created another family joke when Aunt Anne, Mother, and I dubbed the upstairs bedrooms the "Collyer Rooms."[2]

The attic, too, was a very special place. As a child, I was allowed to mount the attic's steep, narrow stairs once a year. As I got older, Aunt Anne let me explore at will. The attic was one large room with a high, bare-raftered ceiling under the hipped roof, lit by a single bare bulb and four elliptical, floor-level windows. The attic was surprisingly bare of objects, although each item was a treasure: a top hat worn by Great-Grandfather John Halliday for Queen Victoria's coronation in 1847, Cousin Donovan Winters's toy trolley car, a box of rocks Uncle Warrington collected in California, and a trunk containing bundles of letters. When they were teenagers, my sister Courtenay and my cousin Warrington sat on the attic floor reading Aunt Anne and Uncle George's love letters.

Grandfather's barn and outbuildings stood on the spacious lot north of his house. A grindstone horse that my brothers, my sister, and I pedaled bicycle-style sat beneath the barn's flared eaves. East of the barn stood a chicken coop and a privy that remained years after the family installed indoor plumbing. When I was ten, I foolishly dropped my treasure-collection shoebox containing the brass buttons from Grandfather's Civil War uniform down the privy hole. In the late 1950s, when Aunt Anne needed money, the lot was sold to the phone company, and Grandfather's house was moved a block away. Today, my treasure trove lies beneath a cement driveway.

When Grandfather died in August 1937, our lawn was lush and redolent with the smells of honeysuckle and lilac and the sounds of mourning doves. A day or two after his death, Aunt Ruth told me that Grandfather had gone away on a long trip, a story that, even at age four, I knew to be a lie. And because Grandmother's physical health was failing, Aunt Anne and Aunt Ruth had decided to tell her the same story as well, a decision with which my mother strongly disagreed. Several months after Grandfather's death, I was led into the small bedroom behind the parlor where

Grandmother was sitting on the edge of her bed. I knew that my aunts were letting me tell her good-bye. That January, Grandmother Brown, who had come to America from England on a sailing ship, also died.

Trips by automobile were my earliest journeys. In 1940, when I was seven, Mother bought a 1939, four-door Pontiac, a car that lasted through my teens and the early driving years of several younger nephews and nieces. When I was young, Mother drove three blocks to Main Street on Saturday afternoons and parked the Pontiac in front of the First National Bank. After sunset, we would walk downtown and spend hours in the car watching the action on the "main drag." In the 1930s and 1940s, Main Street in Pipestone was a vital center for the town and the surrounding farms and villages. Until 10 P.M., people crowded into the stores and bars or leisurely strolled the four-block stretch of Main Street.

Also, at least once a week, Mother and I would drive down to the Great Northern depot to watch incoming trains. At that time Pipestone had four railroads serving nine daily trains, one of which carried passengers. When we saw a passenger staring from a window during the brief time the train stopped to drop off mail, we would make up a story about where that person was going. Mother called these strangers "ships that pass in the night."

Our personal train journeys were exceptional events. In the 1930s, it took four hours to make the sixty-mile trip to Sioux Falls because milk and mail were unloaded along the way. I remember one journey. Mother and I are sitting in the coach's straight-back, rough-velvet seats. A potbelly stove stands in the corner. The train has stopped at Corson, South Dakota, to load milk cans for the city market. As I look out the open door, bright sun casts brilliant light on the cool, green Dakota landscape.

Greater adventures were the rare two-hundred-mile journeys Mother and I occasionally made to Minneapolis. Normal travel by car to Minneapolis today takes three and a half to four hours. In the 1940s, a few demon drivers made the trip in two and a half hours on a two-lane road. Mother was a slow driver who kept an even 15 mph pace in town. When I was learning to drive, she admonished me if I sneaked up to 16 or 20 mph. In the country, where she rarely drove over 40, Mother was a genuine hazard to other drivers. Friends often chided me about Mother's "puttsy" driving.

Pipestone's Main Street was always busy during the 1940s and 1950s. When I was young, people walked downtown on Saturday night to shop, to watch people, and to seek entertainment in the poolhalls, movies, and bowling alleys.

When Alan and Bud were university students in the early 1940s, they sent home soiled clothes that Mother washed and mailed back. Sometimes, however, Mother and I made personal "laundry runs" by car to Minneapolis. My favorite journey occupies a special place in our family's folklore. That day, after leaving Pipestone at 10 A.M. and stopping at a roadside park for our noontime lunch (Mother always packed sandwiches and hard-boiled eggs wrapped in waxed paper) we unhurriedly made our way to Sleepy Eye, a town roughly halfway to Minneapolis. Because Mother never cared to drive at dusk ("the most hazardous time of day to travel," she said), we pulled into the Chief Hotel on Sleepy Eye's Main Street.

This must have been a new experience for me, because I remember the hotel's interior in detail. To the right of the clerk's desk stood a stairwell that led to the rooms on the second floor. Each room had a movable transom and spacious high ceilings. Our room had deep carpeting, flowered wallpaper, and heavy oak furnishings. An unfamiliar, rudimentary device that captured my full attention from the time we entered the room until we left it the following morning was a bracket under the window that held a coiled rope. The rope, Mother told me, was our fire escape.

A large oak table stood in the hotel hallway. A pitcher of ice water and a dozen heavy tumblers, placed rim-side down, sat atop a tapestry tablecloth. Because a hot, dry wind had blown through our open window all evening, about 11 P.M. I became extremely thirsty. Mother feared germs. When I asked if I could get a glass of ice water from the hall, Mother said the glasses might be contaminated because they had come in contact with the (supposedly) unwashed tapestry. Her remedy for thirst — a notion that became a family joke after the Sleepy Eye trip — was to "clack" my tongue to form saliva (never "spit").

After we had finally fallen asleep, we were abruptly awakened by noises coming from a saloon across the street. A party that had begun earlier in the evening was now moving into full gear with the arrival of a country band. With increasing intensity, the party reached a full head of steam before petering out about 3 A.M. The combination of thirst, noise, fear of fire, and lack of sleep kept us awake until dawn. I vaguely remember Mother confronting an indifferent clerk the next morning about the noise and the hotel's (alleged) lack of cleanliness, an action quite in keeping with her character.

Besides the Chief Hotel, the Forum Cafeteria in Minneapolis is another memorable space from my youth. When customers made their way along the stainless steel counters, their images were reflected in the floor-to-ceiling panels of mirrored glass. Noises made by conversing customers and clanging dishes echoed in the lobbylike, high-ceilinged room. Wonderful mashed potatoes and gravy were served in shallow dishes made of cream-colored dinnerware imprinted with the word Forum in bold blue letters.

Great Northern Station in Minneapolis could have held five Forum Cafeterias. As a major passenger and freight hub for Minneapolis, the Dakotas, and Chicago, it was active until the 1960s. The station stood in

Gateway Park, a colorful gathering place for men forced into unemployment by the Depression. When the men gathered outside and within the terminal, their presence added to the visual excitement of entering the station beneath giant Roman arches. Arriving taxis made a pleasant thump-thump as they crossed the brick paving blocks before dropping off passengers in front of the huge, gray-granite portico. In the waiting room, a mural that depicted the signing of an Indian treaty set against a wilderness landscape adorned one wall. The sustained hum of human activity hovered in echoes throughout the room, where the sound of a single footfall carried to the highest corner and there mingled with the thousand other sounds within the station's walls. To a child, there was always an air of excitement and mystery surrounding the journeys of arriving or departing relatives, even those going no farther than southwestern Minnesota.

Before buses became the Twin Cities' major mode of public transportation, riding the streetcars was another adventure for a young person. The oldest cars were yellow wooden boxes rimmed with a bank of windows. In winter, passengers were forced to place their feet on top of the cane seats to keep them from freezing. The signal of an approaching streetcar was the snapping sound of electrical current where the metal poles on the car's roof met the overhead lines.

When I read the works of Aldous Huxley, Thomas Wolfe, and Philip Wylie during my college years, their ideas and feelings intermingled with my own — terminals, trains, and streetcars became engines of romance, and even the common everyday foot errand became a journey. After reading Wolfe's *Only the Dead Know Brooklyn*, I remember how, like Wolfe, I heard and saw, as well as touched and smelled, the mechanical world around me. Thus, for a brief time in the early 1950s, Wolfe's Brooklyn and my St. Paul merged into a single, joyful experience.

In 1942, Mother decided to divide the house into three apartments. Thus, for six years, our house became another space from which to watch passing ships. After Bud left home for the university in 1936, our upstairs became vacant. With only two people at home, conversion from a single-family dwelling to an apartment house was, therefore, fairly simple. Upstairs, Mother had a kitchen installed in one of the bedrooms and a stairway built below the airing deck to serve as a fire escape — a safer exit than the rope ladder at the Chief Hotel!

GREAT NORTHERN PASSENGER STATION,
MINNEAPOLIS, MINN.

GREAT NORTHERN

The Great Northern Station stood at Hennepin Avenue and the Mississippi River in Minneapolis from 1914 to 1978. Designed by Chicago architect Charles Frost, the building's arched pavilions and giant Doric colonnade served as a focal point for the Beaux Arts Gateway Park. Practical as well as monumental, the two arched openings led directly to the concourse, allowing the central bay to be used exclusively as a waiting room. During its peak years, the station served 125 trains a day. Larry Millett, Lost Twin Cities *(St. Paul: Minnesota Historical Society, 1992), 292–93.*

Downstairs, the hallway doors were removed and boarded in to provide space for a new kitchen, which, along with the living room, Mother's bedroom, and my bedroom, formed one downstairs apartment. Although we were cramped for space, Mother and I created a third apartment by converting the sun parlor and dining room into bedrooms and adding a bathroom off the original kitchen. Most of our renters were teachers who stayed a year before moving on, marrying, or reuniting with a soldier-husband. For a time, during the war, our house became a microcosm of the national community.

In 1932, Uncle George Winters built a music studio behind my grandparents' house so Aunt Anne would have a private place to write and to compose music. During the winter of 1943–44, Mother closed up our house to save fuel, and we moved into the studio. One cold January day, I wanted some toys from our own home. The temperature was just above the point at which pipes would freeze. Frost etched my bedroom window,

and the backyard was piled with snow. Slanting afternoon sunlight penetrated a room that now looked as if it belonged to another boy. Even my
toys looked unfamiliar. For a few seconds, I was someone else entering my
own room.

When I was about nine, I began to ask questions about my father. If
Mother ever openly grieved over his death, I have no memory of it. Nor,
sadly, do I remember Mother ever voluntarily telling me stories about my
father. Fortunately, my sister and my brothers remember our father well
and have passed on their cherished memories. According to Bud, Mother
was "devastated" and "completely lost" after my dad's death because he
"protected her from all financial and unpleasant happenings." As for the
reason Mother was silent about her husband in my presence, Bud said,
"She probably wanted to protect you from her sadness by not dwelling on
[Dad's] tragic death, and the terrible loss to you by never knowing him."[3]
My father was one of ten children. When I was a child, only two of his
siblings, Aunt Jessie Genaust and Aunt Alice Martens, were living in Pipestone. For reasons I never have fully understood, my mother rarely social-
ized with the Morgans and often spoke of them in negative terms. Given
this attitude, how ironic it is that my few and brief encounters with the
Morgan family have had a humorous dimension.
When I was about ten, I met Uncle Walter Morgan for the first (and
only) time. That day, I was at Aunt Anne's when Mother frantically
phoned me to rescue her from a "tramp" who was knocking at the door.
When, breathlessly, I entered our house, Mother, now quite embarrassed,
said, "I want you to meet your Uncle Walter." A few years later, when
Walter made a successful one-thousand-foot, free-falling parachute jump
at age seventy-six and the national wire services made my uncle an instant celebrity, Mother, who was embarrassed by the event, hoped no one
would attach Walter's name to ours.[4]
Aunt Jessie died when I was twelve. In what must have been a moment
of peace in her feelings toward the Morgans, Mother offered to hold the
funeral service in our sun parlor. Prior to that day, I had never worn a tie.
As I struggled to tie my tie, Mother asked the undertaker, Fred Walz, if
he would help me. "Sure," Fred said, "but I'd do a better job if Billy would
lie down!"
Regardless of her unspoken feelings toward my father and his family,

Mother was a kind person who tried to fulfill the role of two parents. When I was thirteen, I became the target of the neighborhood bullies. After I repeatedly came home in tears, Mother hired a high school student, Donald Radi, to teach me how to box, using gloves my brothers mailed home at Mother's request. My sparring partner was my best friend, Eddie, Don's youngest brother; our boxing ring was a thicket in the backyard. After touching gloves, Eddie would start to pommel me hard and fast. Before Donald could stop his brother, I would run into the house crying. To Mother's credit, she consistently sent me out again to face my grim opponent.

Besides his boxing ability, Eddie was also a champion at playing marbles. Eddie was the proud owner of several large steelies, the coveted ball bearing shooters that only a few boys owned. Eddie always played "for keeps." Within an hour, I would be cleaned of my marble holdings, making Eddie that much richer in his.

The Radi boys also owned one of Pipestone's largest World War II souvenir collections. By the end of 1944, Alan and Bud were in the army, Stan was in the navy, and Don Radi had enlisted in the marines. Service patches they sent home became our first collectibles. When the men went overseas, German and Japanese insignia, bayonets, helmets, and other paraphernalia began arriving in the mail. When Bud shipped home a German submachine gun, it was intercepted by the postal authorities, and what would have become the neighborhood, if not the town, prize never arrived.

"Johnson's army" was our young boy's version of World War II. My friend Don Johnson organized a unit at the north end of town, while other boys put together a similar outfit at the south end. Our weapon was another Radi creation: a simple wooden rubber-gun. Eddie designed a pine template shaped like a revolver that could be duplicated endlessly on a bandsaw. Ammunition was made from strips of innertube that we stretched around the gun barrel and clamped in place with a clothespin tacked to the gun handle. The proficiency of the Radi revolver led to the development of a rifle model with enough firepower to catapult a rubber strip over our high school. Guns in hand, our armies, Gettysburg-style, stormed a field near the highway overpass, using a high railroad bank as a barricade between the two armies. In this fashion, we fought our own versions of D day, Guadalcanal, and Iwo Jima.

The Pipestone boy armies were involved in the real war as well. Early in the war, the government selected certain citizens to act as block wardens during practice blackouts and others to serve as plane spotters. Local authorities appointed Mother a lieutenant and Aunt Anne a sergeant in the unit that oversaw our neighborhood's monthly blackouts. Their job was to walk around our block and identify houses where someone had absent-mindedly left lights on after the siren had sounded. Mother was also a plane spotter, and I was her assistant. We were provided with a circular cardboard device upon which were drawn the silhouettes of U.S. and enemy aircraft. Had a Stuka, Zero, or Fokker flown over Pipestone, Mother was supposed to contact Sioux Falls, the nearest air force base. Somehow it didn't seem ludicrous to think that the Germans or Japanese might actually bomb southwestern Minnesota.[5]

Pipestone did, in fact, experience one airborne attack, although the aircraft was American. On August 10, 1944, I was standing in front of the Orpheum theater when my professional eye observed a descending P-38 that appeared to be about to strafe Main Street. Diving with a window-rattling roar, the plane leveled off at about the height of our water tower. Fearing the arrival of the inevitable air attack for which the wardens and spotters had prepared, people began pouring out of houses all over town. A few days later, the local paper reported that "residents of Pipestone watched with interest [!] an army plane as it circled low over the city several times. . . . Later it was learned that Flight Officer Roger Dibble, stationed at Coffeyville, Kansas, was the pilot."[6] Roger Dibble, son of the local Chevrolet dealer, was court-martialed, although not discharged, for his unofficial hometown salute.

Homefront warriors contributed to the war effort by making afghans and checker sets, collecting metal and rubber, and planting victory gardens. As fourth graders we spent one hour each morning knitting afghan squares for convalescing veterans in the army hospitals. After purchasing knitting needles at the Ben Franklin store, boys and girls patiently sat working on individual four-by-five-inch squares. Making checkers out of old broomsticks was an alternate project. For years afterward, I imagined a World War I–vintage French hospital where wounded veterans played checkers huddled under our knitted afghans.

During the Depression, even the smallest backyards had been tilled into vegetable gardens. When war broke out, gardening helped people to feel a part of the national effort. Many of us born during the 1930s learned the rudiments of gardening in 4-H clubs like ours, the Pipestone Victory Commandoes. I enlivened the weekly hoeing chore by pretending that certain weeds were "Japs" and others "Nazis."[7]

Collecting metal and rubber was another chore that became a part of our daily routine. After a tin can was emptied, it was carefully washed, de-labeled, and divested of its bottom. The covers were placed inside the can, which was then squashed underfoot and stored in a grocery sack. One Saturday a month, I would leave my sacks on a scale in front of the theater and anxiously await matinee time to see if I had won a free ticket for having the heaviest collection of tin. Since tires were another scarce commodity, rubber drives were as common as those for tin. In response to the demand, Aunt Anne stripped off the rubber edge from her dustpan, thus rendering that instrument useless. For years we joked about Anne's sacrifice for the war effort.

When scrap-drive parades were held, kids toted wagonloads of tin, metal, and rubber down Main Street. Mother had a Victorian cast-iron sewing machine stand (a World War II metal collector's dream) that she let me have for the next scrap-drive parade. We found a cardboard box, tall and wide enough to cover my body, into which we cut a hole for my head and on the side printed "STITCH-UP THE NAZIS." We did not foresee how difficult it would be to maneuver the stand with its tiny, wobbly wheels over the rough pavement. After two blocks of pushing and pulling, I realized I would never get the stand to the end of Main Street. After abandoning the cumbersome object two blocks from home, I continued marching down Main Street in my cardboard costume, its now meaningless message the source of every parade watcher's puzzlement and amusement.

By 1943, almost everyone had a relative or friend in the war. Against the unchanging background of small-town life, the threat of death hung in the air. If we saw a delivery boy, we feared he bore the telegram that began, "The Government regrets to inform you that your son has died [or is missing or has been wounded] in action." Our paperboy, Eddie Radi, carried the August 1944 issue of the *Pipestone County Star* headlining his brother Donald's death in the South Pacific. A few months later, daredevil pilot Roger Dibble went down in flames over Europe. Cousin Homer

Genaust, a marine photographer who had just shot the moving film of the flag raising on Iwo Jima's Mount Suribachi, died at the hands of a flame thrower while seeking refuge in a cave. Brother Alan, a decorated and wounded foot soldier with the First Infantry Division, saw action in North Africa, Sicily, and Europe. Bud, a paratrooper-doctor with the Seventeenth Airborne, was decorated for his jump over the Rhine. Although his age could have kept him home, my oldest brother, Stan, joined the navy in 1944. Mother and I read the papers, listened to the radio, and waited for telegrams.

On Saturday mornings during the war I listened to my favorite radio programs, *Let's Pretend* and *Grand Central Station*. When I heard the narrator of *Grand Central Station* say, "Drawn by the magnetic force of the fantastic metropolis, day and night great trains rush toward the Hudson River . . . flash briefly by the long red row of tenement houses south of 125 Street — then Grand Central Station!" I knew it was almost time to begin my Saturday chores.

Our basement, a gloomy maze of low-ceilinged cinder-block rooms, was the place where I carried out many of my chores. One childhood task involved checking the oil level on the gauge of our oil heater. At night, I used a flashlight or a candle. Going into the furnace room also meant passing by a truly frightening space — the cistern room, its sole access a high window that only a very tall person could see into. We children always imagined someone hiding there. Beyond the cistern lay other rooms — perfect boogeymen hiding places. Because the basement was a reservoir of fear, the secret was to hurry downstairs, do your chores, and beat a path upstairs before someone jumped out at you.[8]

By day, with Mother at my side, the basement laundry room was a rather pleasant space. Saturdays, she washed and I carried out and hung clothes to dry. Once in awhile, Mother would catch her hand in the old-fashioned Maytag wringer. Working outdoors, I would hear a yelp, followed by the sound of the release lever and Mother's voice reassuring me that she was OK.

Stretching curtains was an unwelcome yearly task. This chore involved dipping freshly washed curtains in a bucket of starch and spreading them on a wooden frame. The easel-type frame had rows of sharp points to which the wet, heavy, sticky curtains were attached by means of a rubber roller. The trick was to hold a heavy curtain in one hand while applying the roller with the other. Quite often, I caught a finger between the curtain and the points, adding further pain to this cumbersome process.

An illness that I contracted when I was eleven became the major turning point of my preadolescent years. While playing baseball during the spring of 1944, I developed a sore throat. When the soreness persisted over several days, our family doctor sent a blood sample to Minneapolis, where it was determined that I had developed rheumatic fever. For the next three months, except for trips to the bathroom, I was restricted to complete bed rest. From my bed I followed the news of the European invasion, read through my stack of comic books, and visited with schoolmates who crossed the playground during recess to talk to me through the window.

Besides my bout with rheumatic fever, I also suffered from respiratory problems. To alleviate this condition, Mother would rig a tent by anchoring a sheet to the head- and footboard of my bed. On the floor, under one side of the tent, she placed a steamer kettle that provided a stream of vapor throughout the night.

During the winter of 1944–45, Mother and I both suffered from lung congestion and chronic colds. At our doctor's suggestion, we signed up for a seven-day stay at Mudcura, a sanatorium-spa located near Shakopee, Minnesota.[9]

Situated in a wooded area, Mudcura's red-brick building, spacious front lawn, and circular drive presented an impressive image to a newly arriving patient. In a large dormitory room filled with wooden, zinc-lined, trough-like tables, naked supine patients were covered to their necks with warm mud that was gently emitted from a pipe resembling a cement chute. Over a period of an hour, patients lay under the mud while this crude "natural" process supposedly drew out bodily impurities. I soon grew accustomed to the mud's steaming warmth and deep rich smell — after my fear of total entombment passed.

Behind Mudcura stood a landscaped garden, ornamented with concrete statuary of cherubs and human figures, designed for contemplative walks between treatments. The mud used for treatments was excavated from a large field that lay beyond the garden walls. One day while I was walking around the grounds trying to find something to do, I was introduced to the drayman whose job it was to load the mud and transport it by wagon

This photograph shows Mudcura in Shakopee, Minnesota, as it appeared in the 1940s. After Mudcura closed in 1956 it was used by a Catholic order for a number of years. When I stopped there in 1992, the building was abandoned, partially boarded up, and filled with graffiti and pigeon droppings.

to the sanatorium. The following day, the drayman let me sit beside him as he moved a load in his "mud wagon."

Because I was the only youngster at Mudcura that week, I was an early-morning favorite with many patients but a nuisance in the afternoon, when, according to the rules, everybody was expected to nap for one hour. The window of our cell-like room looked out upon a grove of pines. For half an hour I would battle Mother (who wanted to rest) until she let me go downstairs to play. Play was limited to a tandem swing on the front lawn whose continual squeaky swinging awakened patients. Some of my restlessness surely stemmed from the Mudcura diet. Besides mud treatment and rest, the spa's third rule for good health was a regimen of watery soup, raw carrots, and loads of lettuce. Luckily, Milky Ways and Butterfingers could be purchased in the lobby, creating a source of energy that carried me through the week.

To a twelve year old, Mudcura represented a bizarre trip into the larger world that lay beyond Pipestone, Minnesota, but though Mother swore that her respiratory problems disappeared for six months after leaving Mudcura, I have wondered ever since if the spa was something of a hoax.

Lost among adults, I spent a lonely twelfth birthday at Mudcura riding a tandem swing.

Growing up as an only child, I learned to use my solitude to read, to invent games, to listen to music, and to pursue hobbies — activities that taught me the benefits of introspection and self-motivation. What I did *not* learn was how to compete — a skill other children hone through rough-and-tumble sibling warfare. Furthermore, as a result of my bout with rheumatic fever, I was restricted from pursuing strenuous physical exercise for a period of five years — a regimen that drained my need for competitive activity. As a result, my athletic ability became stunted, and I experienced the acute pain suffered by boys who are always chosen last for sporting events. Between ages eleven to fourteen, I lived with weight gained during my three-month bed rest, pounds that disappeared only after a six-inch growth spurt in the ninth grade.

When I returned to school after my recovery, I fell in love with Norma Brennan, a neighborhood friend, for whom I purchased an eleven-cent, Ben Franklin store ring. I still remember the rush of emotion I felt when I gave Norma the ring. My next-door neighbor, Marilyn Nelson, was another girlfriend. Marilyn's backyard and mine were separated by a cement retaining wall and a row of lilac bushes, where we often played house.

While our playing was generally peaceful, the wall occasionally became a symbol of territorial strife. While Marilyn stood at one end and I at the other, we loudly claimed ownership in the name of our respective families. Thus, our cement barricade became a neighborhood Maginot line.

During my senior year I played the lead role of Stage Manager in our high school production of Thornton Wilder's *Our Town*. My role in Wilder's play, more than any other early experience, helped me to realize the significance of growing up in small-town America. Like Wilder's fictional Grover's Corners, New Hampshire, everything in Pipestone and the surrounding countryside was accessible by bicycle. Our house was located across the street from the school where I attended all twelve grades. To use the playground after school and on weekends, I merely walked out my front door. Main Street, the Orpheum theater, and the ice-cream parlor were only three short blocks away.

Although I was old enough to expand my interests beyond my home, in-house exploration remained my greatest adventure, for there I found a scary basement, bookcases full of yet-to-be-discovered stories, a sunny room to read in, and, on rainy days, secret hiding spaces. Exploring my grandparents' house was my second great adventure. These houses — 310 and 320 Third Avenue Southwest — were the places that inspired my later journeys.

2

My Journey to Field Head, England

From the time I first saw the salt lantern, I dreamed of visiting Field Head, my great-grandmother Anne Kilner Halliday's Cumbria County farm. I began my long-anticipated journey during the winter of 1984 while I was teaching in Northumberland. In early February, my wife, Rosemary, and I took a train from Newcastle to Carlisle and a bus from there to Penrith. As we began the steep ascent into the semimountainous center of Cumbria, we noted snow-footed hedgerows, constructed of tightly woven sticks, that made white, wavy ribbons across the landscape. Although the air was bitterly cold, the warming sun was slowly drying the fields of early morning dew. From our bus window we looked down upon cozy farmhouse porches where strings of onions had been hung to dry. When rain mixed with snow began to fall as we approached the outskirts of Penrith, we wondered if our journey might end there, for we had been warned that a snowstorm could isolate us from Field Head until spring.

Entering Penrith, we discovered a bustling, traffic-clogged market town filled with red sandstone buildings. Prior to our arrival, I had corresponded with George and Eleanor Harrison, owners of Field Head, and from Penrith I phoned to say we hoped to reach the farm the following day. The next morning after the snow stopped we drove to the village of Great Strickland and from there made our way down a paved road that ended at a Y. At the Y, a sign made of metal stick-on (and fall-off) letters read: "F I E D H   D." From the Y, a wagonwide, stonewall-framed dirt road meandered past an unused stone quarry and ended at the farm's courtyard.

As we drove up, the Harrisons were awaiting us at the door. When I saw the farm my aunt had described in "Weighed in the Balance," emotion overwhelmed me, for I was now standing in the courtyard where my great-grandparents began their journey to America. Before sitting down to talk to the Harrisons, I walked across the courtyard and stood by the boundary wall to view the extraordinary vista of the Pennine Chain that spreads out east and north of Field Head across a stretch of wooded wasteland.

Sitting at the Harrisons' kitchen table, I began asking questions that would link the stories I had heard as a child to the reality of the farm itself. In "Weighed in the Balance," Aunt Anne Winters had written that her grandmother, Anne Kilner Halliday, had told her that the kitchen floor at Field Head was cool and that John Kilner, Anne's father, had covered the stairs leading to the second floor with oak slabs because they had become so worn with use (see appendix 1). Eleanor Harrison verified these details and said that an orchard spring that runs beneath the house keeps the kitchen naturally cool. She added that John Kilner's oak boards still lie beneath the modern carpeting.

When I walked outside again, I discovered — and later studied in detail — that Field Head was designed with human and animal shelters close at hand, a plan that makes circulation accessible while shutting out a harsh climate and unwelcome visitors. Although the farmhouse interior seems relatively unchanged from the time when Kilners lived there, the exterior has been stuccoed and a glassed-in porch added as a place to leave muddy boots.

Verifying the validity of family stories concerning the Kilners proved more difficult. Some stories, however, stand on their own merit. In "Weighed in the Balance," Aunt Anne wrote that the Kilners were members of the Church of England but that many of their renters were

The view from Field Head toward the Pennine Chain reveals the idyllic beauty of rural Cumbria. Except for the highlines, this view appears unchanged from the time the Kilners lived at Field Head. Looking northeast is an unobstructed view of Cross Fell, the highest of a series of fells (a stretch of elevated wasteland) that makes up the Pennine Chain. Although the ground was saturated with mist and rain, bright, sun-drenched clouds rolled across the fell all day.

Methodists. One day when John stopped to collect rent, he was told the family had no money and little to eat. John decided, however, to wait and chat awhile. As they talked, the renter's young son kept pointing to the oven, saying "Tate noven." When the mother tried to hush her son, John said, "Open the door to satisfy him." Sure enough, there was a "tate" (cake) in the oven, suggesting to John an ample larder, or at least more provisions than the renters had revealed. According to Aunt Anne, her grandmother always believed that Methodists could never be trusted.

Between 1899 and her death in 1915, Great-Grandmother Anne Kilner Halliday lived with her daughter and son-in-law and their children in Pipestone. Every summer afternoon, Anne Kilner and her daughter, Mary Halliday Brown, set out their linen-covered walnut table and served tea on the north lawn. This ritual suggests the cultural habits and high aspirations inherited from a long line of quasi-aristocratic landowners. A great-grandson, Stan Morgan, claims that the Kilner-Hallidays were lazy. An-

Field Head's farmhouse is part of a range of outbuildings. The stable/barn (right) is constructed of gray coursed limestone trimmed with reddish sandstone ashlar. William Kilner's initials and the year "1796" appear in the small square block above the stable door.

other great-grandson, the late Warrington W. Winters, wrote that John Kilner "never worked a day in his life, except to read the Riot Act."[1]

Aunt Anne Winters supported the notion that the Kilners were rural aristocrats. She said that John Kilner wore knee breeches, long white stockings, and low shoes with silver buckles. When he tore a stocking, John forced his daughters to darn it so "the mend must never show." While John expected his daughters and servants to fulfill their duties, he was lenient toward his only son, William. Since John was also a cellist and a patron of a string quartet, music was undoubtedly more important to him than farming.

According to Aunt Anne, John Kilner hired maids at the lowest possible wage and made his daughter Anne overseer. Field Head's day laborers were paid two shillings for a fourteen-hour shift, and their hours were so long that lanterns had to be used in the morning and at night. (In "Weighed in the Balance," Aunt Anne noted parenthetically: "No wonder there were wars and rebellions.") Although Anne Kilner was forced to work hard, she was, nevertheless, her father's favorite child because she had the nerve to stand up to him. Given the fact that John was strict

Attached to the house (left) is the stable/barn (now a garage) and the granary (formerly the byre). The Harrisons use the granary for a milking parlor and hay storage. An American-type metal building (far right) closes the courtyard between west and east ranges.

with his other daughters, Anne Kilner's behavior must indeed have been unique.

On this busy Cumbrian farm, cheese tubs were kept in the spring-fed milk house, and the meat house sheltered butchered geese. Although food was plentiful, the Kilners rarely served butter and meat at the same meal. Hired help sat in a separate dining area, and, until they learned proper manners, children were not allowed to eat at their parents' table. Recalcitrant children sometimes were forced to stand at meals. Aunt Anne wrote that this was the way English parents "hardened" their children.

No one knows when Kilners first came to Great Strickland, although records indicate they began arriving in the area sometime during the sixteenth century. Brothers John and Thomas Kilner appear in the 1538 Morland church register. Verifiable family connections to Great Strickland and Field Head begin with William Kilner, who married Elizabeth Rowlinson of Dufton in 1787. The initials "W. K.," inscribed in the stable wall, belong to this William, builder and administrator of Field Head during the decades bridging the end of the eighteenth and the beginning of the nineteenth centuries. At that time, the farm anchored the "head" of twelve

Field Head's east range contains a workshop, cowshed, and calf pen. In design, choice of materials, and craft, this building appears to be contemporaneous with the west range.

fields, each rented by one family. As landowners, William and his descendants collected rent from farmers (including Methodists) who lived and worked at Field Head.[2]

When I was a child, I heard a story that has circulated among family members for several generations. The story has to do with the Kilners' unexpected departure from Field Head about 1871. Kilner descendants on both sides of the Atlantic are presently researching this "lost fortune" story. When John Kilner died in 1849, his son, William, inherited the estate. According to the story I heard as a child, William lost Field Head while gambling at cards. In "Weighed in the Balance," Aunt Anne alluded to the gambling story — "a sad tale I'll tell you later if I have the courage, and feel it right to divulge family secrets" — to tease my imagination. On my twenty-eighth birthday (*now* I was old enough to hear the truth!) Aunt Anne wrote me:

> I don't know whether you know how the estate passed from *our hands*, to [our relatives] the Courtenays. I don't like to tell you as it always hurt Grandma H[alliday], but by now she doubtless knows that many such things happened. Great-Grandpa Kilner gambled, alas! and lost the

estate. Poker? It was to go out of Kilner hands for one generation only, as it was entailed. But I believe that no K[ilner] ever got it back.[3]

When I mentioned the gambling incident to the Harrisons, they responded with great interest, for they had heard the story too. My English relatives, Dorothy Smith and David Fallowfield, for several years have been researching Kilner family history. As a child, Dorothy was told that her ancestors "had been well off, but had lost their money, always rather mysterious — drink, gambling, but nothing concrete." When she was older, Dorothy learned that around 1871, William, his wife, Elizabeth, and several of the Kilner children had moved to a cottage in Patterdale, a village near Field Head. In the 1871 Patterdale census, Dorothy learned that William, fifty-three, earned two pounds a month as a lead-mine worker, and that his son John, thirteen, labored as a lead-ore washer. (According to the 1881 census, William Kilner was still in the mines.) At about the time of the loss of Field Head, another son, William, and a daughter, Barbara Ann, who was Dorothy Smith's grandmother, moved to the village of Newby to live with an aunt. Dorothy told me that her grandmother was forced to work as a domestic but that when she turned nineteen she left her job and got married. Dorothy was told as a child that John Kilner never forgave his father for losing Field Head.[4]

Oral tradition and census records seemingly corroborate the lost fortune story. Dorothy Smith's research shows that the Kilner family was forced to change its life-style, perhaps because William Kilner gambled.[5] For over two hundred years, Kilners plowed the land beneath the Pennine Chain. Field Head is an active farm today, built upon the independent, self-reliant, and hard-working habits of the Harrison family. The landscape, buildings, and daily work cycle of these farmers connect Field Head to the distant past where Kilners once worked and dreamed.

My Journey to Ecclefechan, Scotland

Following my journey to England, I traveled to Scotland to learn firsthand about the stories I had heard about my Halliday ancestors. In the Scottish Lowlands, an hour's drive from Field Head, lies the village of Ecclefechan, birthplace of my great-grandfather John Halliday and a town well known as the home of philosopher and writer Thomas Carlyle. When I arrived in Ecclefechan on a dreary February day in 1984, I had scant information about John Halliday's life in Scotland except for the oral stories · my aunt recorded in "Weighed in the Balance." According to Aunt Anne, John's mother was so frugal that to save leather she carried her shoes when she left the house. To provide fuel for their fireplace, the Hallidays cut and dried blocks of peat from a nearby bog. "It was a good thing they had [peat], as they were quite lacking in money," Anne wrote. Though poor, the family was "perhaps . . . very wealthy in mind and spirit as so many Scotch people are," she added.

John Halliday was a man of many talents. As a child, he studied his "bukes" (Aunt Anne's rendering of his pronunciation of "books") often having to hide to read when he was supposed to be doing his chores. For a short time when he was a youth, John attended medical school with funds provided by an uncle. When his benefactor unexpectedly died, John had to leave school to follow the shoemaker's trade. Besides working as a tradesman, John sang, played the violin and bass viol, and made stringed instruments. Until he was ninety, he could quote from memory long passages from Robert Burns, Shakespeare, and the Bible.

Sometime during the 1840s, John Halliday left home and moved to England, where he set up a shoemaker's shop in Great Strickland. Although he was a Presbyterian, John attended St. Andrew, the Anglican church in Penrith, where he sang in the choir and played the violin. When John Kilner, another St. Andrew parishioner, recognized John's talent, he invited the shoemaker-musician to play in his string quartet at Field Head. There, John met and courted Anne Kilner.

John and Anne's courtship story is an essential piece of our family's oral history. Many times as I was growing up I heard Aunt Anne and Mother say that while John Kilner admired John Halliday's musicianship, he tried to discourage his daughter from marrying a "lowly shoemaker," especially one of Scottish birth. However, the headstrong Anne told her father that John's character would tip the scales if weighed against the values of her other suitors.[1] During the summer of 1847, Anne and John were married, and the following October Anne gave birth to a daughter, Mary, at Field Head. John Kilner must have been forgiving, because he soon built the salt lantern house for the young family in nearby Great Strickland.[2]

I traveled to Scotland to find the place where John Halliday lived prior to leaving for England. As much as I wanted to see the village, my interest began to wane as soon as I crossed the flat and barren border where crisscrossing highlines and small damp cottages dotted the Lowland landscape. Even the place-names, such as Cargo and Ashyard Crescent, mirror this desolate region. As the bus approached Ecclefechan, it began to drizzle and then to rain.[3] When I saw the village, I began to feel depressed, lonely, and filled with a strange sense of apprehension. I did not want to be trapped in that dreary place, so I immediately checked the bus schedule to be sure that travel was possible the following Sunday.

After finding a bed-and-breakfast, I walked in the rain to a nearby churchyard, where I had an experience that is forever engraved in my mind. In the churchyard I found thick, six-foot-high stones that seemed to press down upon the people buried beneath them. While I stood in the rain, surrounded by stones marked "Halliday," I heard a dull, insistent sound from a nearby concrete plant. The sight of the huge damp stones and the sound of the monotonous machine reinforced my desire to escape this strange and lonely place.

Ecclefechan's physical layout adds to the village's dreariness. Most of the town lies between the arms of a V formed by an old army road to the west and the modern A74 highway to the east. Ecclefechan's major buildings climb a low hill along the older road, which once carried border raiders south into Northumberland. Most travelers merely bypass Ecclefechan by taking the A74.

In an attempt to dispel my growing depression brought on by the village's visual dullness and its dismal weather, I sought out a friendly face and found the local Presbyterian minister, George Irving, and his wife, Maybell. During the next two days, George drove me around the countryside, introducing me to his Halliday parishioners and helping me search neighboring graveyards. Allen Cunningham, the retired village registrar of deeds, combed parish records for references to John Halliday. Although we found the names of hundreds of Hallidays, living and deceased, who lived in or near Ecclefechan, Great-Grandfather John Halliday's name never appeared. On Sunday, disappointed but happy to leave the village, I took a bus and returned to Northumberland.

As I was planning to leave England, I had one more chance to visit Scotland. A week after my journey to Ecclefechan, I found the following item in the Dumfrieshire Middlebie parish book in the Edinburgh Registry Office. The barely legible entry read: "December 3, 1815, William Halliday and Janet Thomson his wife in Brownmuir baptised John." I was sure, from this small item, that I had found my great-grandfather's name. Unfortunately, I could not return to Ecclefechan to search for Brownmuir, but later, back home in Minnesota, while studying an ordnance survey map, I found Brownmoor, a farm about two miles southeast of Ecclefechan.[4] Four years passed, however, before I could return to Scotland.

My experience at Brownmoor in 1988 was more encouraging than my earlier visit to Ecclefechan. My English relative and guide, David Fallowfield, using his authority as a Cumbria County policeman, had checked with authorities in advance of my visit, locating a renter, John Thomson, who was

Highway A74 splits as you enter Ecclefechan. In the far distance, middle right, is Ecclefechan Parish Church. Thomas Carlyle's boyhood home can be seen in the extreme right corner. The large cattle shelter (left) is one of Ecclefechan's few modern structures.

awaiting our arrival. As David, my son Bill, and I drove up Brownmoor's long entrance driveway, I was immediately reminded of the driveway to the farm near Lake City, Minnesota, where John and Anne Kilner Halliday later settled. I felt sure that I had found John Halliday's birthplace, especially when I saw the similarity between Brownmoor's landscape and the bluff country above Lake City. Now I was convinced that the Cumbrian and Scottish Lowland landscapes had influenced my great-grandparents as they selected sites and built their homes across America.

The Brownmoor farmstead consists of a well-preserved nineteenth-century Georgian house and a group of older service buildings. The farmhouse, like the one near Lake City, stands at the end and to the left of a long driveway. The house is a rather tall, three-bay structure, with a narrow, projecting entranceway. Its walls are built of quarry-faced stone, heavily pebble-dashed and painted white, with window frames trimmed in

The Hallidays' Georgian farmhouse at Brownmoor is built of stone and finished in pebble-dash. Many farmhouses in the area have corbelled dormers, and though Brownmoor lacks this feature, the roofline design is Flemish in feeling.

black. Windowsills, eaves trough, and entranceway are also trimmed in black to suggest half-timbering. Twin dormers and chimneys project from the roofline. The ghost line of an attached room appears on the east facade, showing the presence of an older, one-story, thirty-foot-wide structure, mirroring the roof form of an American saltbox. Mr. Thomson said this missing unit must have been an attached one-room-and-pantry cottage.

The farmhouse interior has been remodeled in recent times. At one time, the living room may have been a one-room cottage, similar to the one now removed. Although it has gone through many changes, the room's cavelike appearance — a low-lying fireplace and small window openings — evokes a strong sense of mid-nineteenth-century cottage life. An added lean-to, containing a kitchen, hallway, parlor, and three upstairs bedrooms, is connected to the house on the west.

A few feet behind the farmhouse a courtyard links the house to the range of service buildings. During our visit, David, who has studied rural buildings in northern England, said the service buildings at Brownmoor

This view of Brownmoor's courtyard shows the two ranges that served the multiple functions required of an active farm. Today, it is impossible to determine how this space was originally used. (The back and side walls of the farmhouse can be seen on the far right.)

may date back to the 1700s. The range buildings include (from east to west) four attached rooms (part of which also may have been domestic quarters), a byrelike section at right angles to the other rooms, and a mill-shed (sometimes called an "engine house") at the far west end. The mill-shed originally housed a space where grain was ground by a horse walking in a circle around a central post. Within a few feet south of the house stands another barn of about the same vintage as the service buildings.

While I was studying the buildings, Brownmoor's owner, Drew Clark, drove into the courtyard bearing an old oilcloth map. Mr. Clark, John, and I got down on the living room floor and spread out this prize, an early map of the Brownmoor site. At the top of the map it said: "Plan of the Estate of Luce Comprehending the Farms of Meinbank, Whins, Luce, and Woodside and also the Lands and Farms of Parkgate, Williamwood, Allalie, and Brownmuir Pendicles Belonging to the Trustees of the Late Gen. and Mrs. Dirom of Mt. Annan."[5]

Mr. Clark said that General Dirom died in 1830. Assuming the map was drawn to settle Dirom's estate, Brownmoor can be dated with certainty to

1830, plausibly with an even earlier date of construction. One section (19) of the Dirom map shows a shaded area that resembles the outline of the service buildings extant today. Next, I tried to locate names to attach to the Brownmoor site. The 1801 Annan parish census records the following names under "Brownmoor Limeworks": William Holiday, Jean Scott, Thomas Holiday, William Holiday, and Jenet Holiday.[6] I also found a "Brown Muir" and nearby lime quarries on a later map.[7] When Mr. Clark told me there were quarries in the nearby woods, I wondered if the quarry workers named in the census were my Halliday ancestors. Were William and Jenet (Janet Thomson?) Holiday John Halliday's parents? Did they live in a cottage at Brownmoor?

I like to imagine that, given his love of reading, his medical experience, and his craftsman's skills, the road lay open for Great-Grandfather John Halliday outside the rigors of the Brownmoor quarry works.[8]

4

The Hallidays' Journey to America

When I was young, I was fascinated by a painting that I found in a book that lay on a table in our living room. Ford Madox Brown's somber figures in *The Last of England*, according to my mother, held a similar interest for her grandmother, Anne Kilner Halliday, because the painting reminded her of her own journey to America.

As I prepared for my England journey, I had in mind three artifacts: Ford Madox Brown's painting, Great-Grandmother Anne Kilner Halliday's salt lantern, and the journal John Halliday kept during his family's voyage to America in 1855. From the time that my cousin Warrington Winters published an excerpt from our great-grandfather's journal, I began searching for the original document.[1] Through family contacts I found relatives in New York State with whom I had a chance to visit in 1994. There, for the first time, I held the leather-bound, silver-clasped journal that John Halliday carried from England.[2] From the original journal and published excerpts I was able to piece together the story of the Hallidays' journey to America.

Ford Madox Brown painted The Last of England *in 1855, the same year the Hallidays sailed from Liverpool. According to one critic, the work was undertaken after Brown saw a friend off for Australia and reflects Brown's "own depressed thoughts of emigration." Courtesy of the Tate Gallery.*

On August 4, 1855, the Hallidays' sailing ship, the *St. Patrick*, left Liverpool, bound for Quebec, carrying steerage and second-class passengers. John and Anne Halliday and their children, Mary, eight, and William, nine, were among the second-class passengers. Like the emigrants in Brown's painting, the Hallidays knew that never again would they see John's family or Anne's brother and three sisters. Besides carrying passengers, the ship was also a carrier of death, for during the forty-four-day journey, at least nine children, the majority from steerage, died of typhus, inflammation of the lungs, or cases diagnosed as cholera.

Because the *St. Patrick* ran into calm weather with intermittent winds for the first twenty-five days, the ship did not reach Newfoundland until August 28. On that day, with a fresh breeze blowing from the north, the captain ordered passengers to air their beds on deck, a process, according to the journal, that "render[ed] the place much sweeter." As the wind died down again that evening, John noted that "another child [was] committed to the deep." Passengers became more restless and uncomfortable when the *St. Patrick* made only eighteen miles during the next day and night. On the 29th, John recorded in his journal: "yesterday we could scarcely keep heat walking. Today we can hardly keep cool sitting." As the ship was running behind schedule and the food supply was rapidly depleting, passengers who earlier had refused to eat common oatmeal and biscuits from the ship's store now began to eat anything available. During this critical period, John kept his mind off food by taking instructions in navigation: "[I] had a look through the Quadrant and a lesson from the captain as to the mode of using it. He also shewed me the manner of working out the observation which is done in very few figures. We are in Lat 46′ 12″ having just made 18 miles south since yesterday. Heartless work."[3]

Three days later, a driving rain and fierce west winds forced the ship to leave its northwesterly course and turn even farther south. If Quebec were to be reached at all now, John felt, "[we] must submit to the will of Heaven." In spite of adverse weather, lack of food, and recurring fights among the sailors, the crew and passengers found sport by searching passengers' clothing for lice. During what John called a "hunt," a sailor turned his deck hose on a lice-ridden "German or Dutch[man]," and "the cold water proved most effectual, causing both huntsman and game to disappear as if by magic." The next day,

> one of the grey ones [a louse] was discovered on a lads coat. One of the passengers desired him to go down and take it off, the captain who was present ordered him to take off his coat and do it gently. This was done and then he ordered him to heave [the louse] overboard repeating the word 5 or 6 times causing much laughter increasing it by adding that it was large enough to bait a codfish hook. So that with one thing and an-

other the time passes swiftly away with those in health among which thanks be to an all merciful God are me and mine. (August 31)

A few days short of a month out of Liverpool, with the wind blowing fiercely and the ship making only five miles a day, John wrote that the ship's supply of sugar and butter was nearly spent and their own provisions almost gone, "and we still a 1000 miles from the end of our journey. Glorious position. All in good health and spirits though. As soon as [young son] Wm made his appearance on deck this morning the captain laid hold of his cap saying now the cap's mine I have seen land. Wm said no not till I'm on't." The final entry that day reads: "Another child has just died in the Stearage" (September 1).

During the following week, the ship once again was becalmed because hot, westerly winds blew night and day. In the sailors' opinion, there was "a Jonas on board," to which John added, "It is indeed strange that out of 31 days we should only have had 2 days of favourable wind. The children are both complaining. Hot and feverish. We have had a very sleepless night" (September 3).

Several journal references to doctoring strongly support the story told in our family that John once attended medical school. When his own children fell ill, John dispensed pills that may have led to their recovery, and throughout the journal he is highly critical of the diagnoses made by the ship's doctor. On September 8, John wrote: "The doctor who is a *rime* customer and much troubled with the disease called laziness is much afraid of ships fever and says it is already in the Stearage. I [too] would have been alarmed had he not prophesied measales, scarlatina, small pox etc, as soon as we were in the fogs of Newfoundland[,] none of which has happened as yet." By *rime*, I imagine that John meant "frost-covered." In his opinion the ship's doctor was too old ("hoary") or too far removed from up-to-date medical knowledge to make correct diagnoses. Later, when the first child in a second-class cabin became ill from what the doctor called cholera, John noted that "from the symptoms I cannot agree with him."

Because John had to fetch water below decks, he became familiar with conditions in steerage. He wrote: "the stench was dreadful and the dirt about one-half inch deep many of the passengers being of such filthy habits as to make water on the floor. All the efforts of the captain and officers to improve them are unavailing." During a storm, a particularly heavy lurch caused the steerage chamberpots to overturn. These "*'Nosegays'* alias Chamber pots" produced such a stench, John said, it would have "poisoned a pole cat" (September 5).

Six weeks out of Liverpool, the wind began to blow in the ship's favor, but now there was little food left. The Hallidays were out of ham and butter, and salt beef purchased from the ship's store "did not belie its name being as salt as brine and as tough as leather." In addition to the food problem, typhus had broken out, carrying the eighth child to its grave. Fortunately, the ship was making headway up the St. Lawrence River toward Grosse Isle, a quarantine station in the St. Lawrence estuary.[4] As they moved upstream, John recorded his impressions of the river, sky, and surrounding landscape: "We are now fairly in the [St. Lawrence] river a magnificent river it is. Were such a river to run through England it would leave very small parings in the widest of it and across from Whitehaven to Durham it would require to borrow a good deal from the German ocean" (September 12). Two days later he wrote: "A splendid morning far exceeding all my ideas of the American climate. I have often read of Italian skies but if they excel these they must be blue glorious indeed . . . we are again moving though slowly towards our destination. Thanks be to God we are all well again" (September 14). As the ship neared shore, John noted: "The river had narrowed greatly [and] was as smooth as glass and the banks on each side [were] literally covered with houses all white with small patches of clearings. . . . Among all the beauties of the place and they are not a few I missed the green fields of England" (September 14).

The beauty of the landscape was soon forgotten, however, as new problems arose. On the morning of the 15th, officers from Grosse Isle came aboard and quarantined the passengers for a two- to three-day period. That afternoon, a steamboat arrived to take passengers to the station, where, to John's consternation, no provisions were available: "Many had nothing to eat and nothing to purchase with. Consequently [the passengers'] case was anything but enviable. . . . darkness found us on a strange land with seemingly no one to direct us where to go." When the Hallidays reached shore, they found that the wooden sheds used for housing passengers were locked because the quarantine officer had retired to dinner. John sardonically recorded his first experience in the New World: "the hungry cattle must wait till his highness had finished [his meal] . . . when we inquired if there were any provender for hungry bellies [the returning officer] said there was plenty of food in the store for money and that we could please ourselves whether we eat or starved. Wherever we go *money* is our *friend*."[5]

The next morning John arose and bought warm bread and six pounds of potatoes. For the first time in weeks, the family had tea with sugar in it. After breakfast, John took a walk about the island, which he described as "all rock but covered with trees, chiefly the pine tribe, silver, fir, spruce, white, red pine, plenty of juniper . . . it is a beautiful place."[6]

My Journey to Checkerberry Village, Vermont

According to family stories, the Hallidays lived in Canada during their first winter in North America but moved to Wisconsin sometime between 1856 and 1860. According to the 1860 federal census, John, Anne, William, and Mary Halliday resided near the village of Tiffany in Rock County, Wisconsin, where, like many pioneers, they may have rented land or worked for another farmer until they could afford to purchase land of their own.

During their Wisconsin years, Mary Halliday met her future husband, Warrington Brown, who, in 1857, had moved with his parents, Jason and Sarah Brown, from Vermont to the nearby village of Center. The story of my grandfather Warrington Brown's family begins with his maternal ancestors, the Stannards of St. Albans, Vermont, and the Brown family of Checkerberry Village, Vermont.

In the summer of 1924, my grandfather attended a national convention of the Grand Army of the Republic in Boston. When the convention ended, he took a train to Vermont to visit places he had left when he was twelve. The journal Grandfather kept during that journey left detailed notes of the following places he knew as a child: his grandfather Amos Brown's farm near Checkerberry Village, Chittenden County, where he was born; Great-Grandfather Samuel Stannard's house, built in 1794 in Franklin County; and the home of his maternal grandparents, Samuel and Rebecca Stannard, near Georgia Center.

The journal reveals my grandfather's painful awareness of the changes that had taken place since the 1850s. When he describes his great-grandparents' Franklin County house, a sense of loss underlies his description of the structure's details:

> Log house covered with siding. Two large front rooms. Two large back rooms, three small rooms & large loft. Rafters 8 x 10 in. thick, round logs, 8 feet apart and boarded with 3 inch hand hewed plank. Spiked with blacksmith made spikes. Rafters pinned at the top and on plates with oak pins. Main part of house stands up in strong shape but shingles blown off. Old stairs very narrow and nearly purpendetlur. Old wells and one old Barn. Apple, plum and peach orchards all gone. One very old thorn Locas [locust] tree in front of house close in between 2 front doors 3 ft. thru.

Then, when he visits his mother's birthplace, the Samuel and Rebecca Stannard home near Georgia Center, he writes that "very sacred memories" are stirred while standing in the room "where [his] saintly mother was borne." Here, he sees the "same old rooms" where his grandparents sat, and the place where he "wrastled and tusseled" with his "Unkel Daniel" until his grandmother made him leave the house to do his chores.[1]

Nostalgia turns to despair when Warrington visits his own birthplace, Grandfather Amos Brown's "grand old farm," which he found radically changed. Initially he is impressed with the apparent prosperity and technical progress he sees in the surrounding countryside: "No stumps in sight. Threshing a nice crop of grain. People look very prosperous. Buildings very nice. Threshing with a small separator [run by a] small gas engine." But Warrington discovers that most of his grandfather's buildings have been moved or destroyed; and while he is able to locate sites that he can recall from childhood, like the "old hill where [he] knocked [his] tooth out," most of the cultivated landscape has returned to a state of wildness:

Beautiful spring and gorge on east so densley grown to pines you can hardly find the place. Old orchard all gone but 2 scrubby apple trees. Several old rotten stumps. One enormus old hard maple tree where 4 were planted when I was 3 years old. Nearly all fruit and all nut trees gone. Pasture grown up to pine, seader [cedar], and spruce trees. Very sad looking sight. I am glad and yet I am sad. To see things run down so. More Christ and less red rum and things would not be so sad.

With Grandfather Brown's journal in hand, I set out to search for physical traces of his Vermont heritage. Although even greater changes had taken place in the landscape of northwestern Vermont over the ensuing sixty years, nevertheless I was able to locate material evidence of the lives of the Stannard and Brown families in Chittenden and Franklin Counties. Although I could document with certainty only one house associated with our family's material heritage (the home of Sarah Stannard Brown's brother, Civil War general George J. Stannard), I also discovered through deed searches, atlases, and site visits two additional houses that once may have belonged to members of the Brown family.

The Brown and Stannard sites lie along U.S. Highway 7 between Colchester-Milton and St. Albans. This older highway crisscrosses Interstate 89, winding through lush countryside that took me back into the 1870s, and, on county roads, to an earlier period. "Progress," however, is at work everywhere. By the year 2000, Highway 7 between Burlington and the Canadian border is destined to become a single commercial strip. From the perspective of superhighway 89, I caught only momentary glimpses of the grandeur of Lake Champlain as I sped north toward Canada.

I followed my family's heritage by moving north along Highway 7 from Checkerberry Village and Milton to St. Albans. I discovered that Checkerberry Village still roughly resembles its nineteenth-century physical layout, where several early Greek Revival houses, including the Stagecoach Inn (now restored as a home), face the original village park. In terms of my own heritage, however, my greatest discovery was the recently restored 1816–1870 Checkerberry cemetery, where I found the graves of four of Warrington Brown's siblings. According to the tombstones, Lelila and Losey died in 1852 and twins Eliza and Alma in 1853.[2] It is hard to imagine the grief of losing four children within the span of one year.

As I searched further for traces of the Brown family, I discovered deed

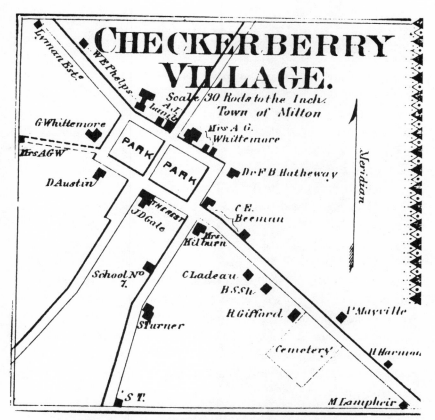

Checkerberry Village, Vermont, still retains many of the same elements, including roads leading away from houses scattered around a village green, that appear in the Atlas of Chittenden County, Vermont. *New York: Beers, Ellis, & Soule, 1869.*

records, an atlas, and maps that helped me in my quest. Deed records in the Milton town hall show that Amos Brown owned large sections of land around Checkerberry Village. In 1984, four sections of land that once belonged to Amos were relatively undeveloped and remained in a state of wildness. Cobble Hill, the major landmark on this landscape, is a tree-covered elevation that overlooks property formerly owned by the Brown family. According to Ivan Sanderson, a local resident who volunteered to guide me in the Milton area, observers who stood on this hill in 1814 during the Battle of Plattsburgh could see cannon smoke from ships locked in combat on Lake Champlain.[3]

The only structure appearing in section 17 on a ca. 1820 proprietor's map is a dot labeled "E. Reynolds" on the 1869 atlas map. Amos Brown sold this section to Horace Loomis in 1828. On the Reynolds site I found a one-and-one-half-story Greek Revival house with an attached kitchen and woodshed ell. Two large "husband and wife" maple trees, five feet in diameter, stood on the front lawn. In 1852, Amos Brown deeded lots in sections 15 and 31 to his son Jason for a thousand dollars. My grandfather's parents, Jason and Sarah Brown, and their six children most likely lived in the house labeled "E. P. Herrick" on the 1869 atlas map. The land deeds, maps, and atlases dovetail with Warrington's journal notation: "Old Roberts farm [was sold] to Jason Brown and sold by Jason Brown to Herick." The Herrick site was a vacant lot in 1984; across the road to the north, a trailer park sat on section 14.

I narrowed the search for my grandfather's birthplace, described in his journal as the "1400-acre Amos Brown farm," to a strip of land in sections 13 and 14 southeast of Checkerberry Village. An 1857 survey map shows a structure labeled "A. Brown" about a mile southeast of Checkerberry Village on the Stage Road.[4] One-half mile beyond the "A. Brown" site is a structure designated as belonging to "G. Brown." From the evidence of the maps, it appears that Amos Brown and his sons, Jason and George, owned houses and large tracts of land near Checkerberry Village between the 1820s and late 1850s.

My attempt to document the "G. Brown" site ended somewhat humorously. When I asked the man who came to the door about early occupants, he said, "The house is not that old," and shut the door in my face. I had better luck with his neighbor, David De Mag, a man in his late twenties who lives in what may be the "A. Brown" house, or at least a house on the site of my grandfather's birthplace. Mr. De Mag works in town and lives with two Dobermans and a cub cougar. Although he worked the day I planned to do my fieldwork, De Mag, unlike his neighbor, allowed me to leisurely study his house and property while he was away.

Although I was unable to judge the distance between Checkerberry Village and the "A. Brown" structure from the unscaled 1857 map, I not only photographed and measured the De Mag house but also combed the wild area facing the Stage Road between the house and Checkerberry Village, searching for physical evidence of past habitation. De Mag's house stands in almost pristine isolation and has an unobstructed view of Cobble Hill. My exploration of the ground north of his house revealed an area of over-

The Brown/Reynolds house in Checkerberry Village stands on a lot Amos Brown sold in 1828. A comparison of this structure with photographs of other contemporary Vermont houses places this building within the era 1820 to 1840.

grown vegetation, including young trees, plants, and ferns, where I found depressions resembling former building sites: a two-foot-wide depression denoting a foundation footing and, nearby, a thirty-five-by-forty-foot depression indicating a possible barn site. Following the 1857 map, I would place the site of the Amos Brown farm within the strip of land directly north of, and possibly including, the De Mag house. This strip of land had retained as much of its wild, nineteenth-century character as any site I have seen in my family searches, including the Mississippi River bluffs above Lake City, Minnesota (see chapter 8) and the unspoiled "Halliday Hill" area near Sanborn, North Dakota (see chapter 10).

The "Reynolds" and the De Mag houses are similar in style to family structures that I have studied in Minnesota. Like the John and Anne Kilner Halliday house, Florence township, Goodhue County, Minnesota (chapter 8) and the Warrington and Mary Brown homestead, Grange township, Pipestone County, Minnesota (chapter 9), the Vermont houses are vernacular Greek Revival in style and follow a hall-and-parlor floor plan.

The Amos Brown/De Mag house in Checkerberry Village is a good example of a vernacular Greek Revival structure. A fieldstone foundation may date to the Amos Brown era.

The one site where I could find a direct family link is the Gen. George Jerrison Stannard farm on Highway 7 near Milton, owned in 1984 by Mr. Sanderson, who lived next door. During my Vermont journey, Sanderson permitted me to study the Stannard house inside and out. The Greek Revival house was built in 1823 and purchased by the general following his service during the Civil War. Although the interior has been extensively remodeled, the house retains much of its original exterior appearance.[5] (A biography of General Stannard is found in appendix 3.)

The day I completed my fieldwork, I stopped to say good-bye to Ivan Sanderson. Ivan, more than anyone else, helped me to understand many aspects of the social history of northwestern Vermont. At the time of Ivan's birth in 1915, his neighbors were self-sufficient cattle farmers. As my grandfather observed in 1924, industry had introduced one-cylinder gas engines that lightened farmers' chores. When Ivan showed me an engine that he and his friends were restoring, he said, "People today don't even know what they are!"

General Stannard purchased this 1823 Greek Revival house after completing his Civil War service. An early photograph shows such features as a five-bay facade, twin chimneys, unpainted clapboard siding, sash windows, and rear lean-to. In 1984 I discovered that the house lies in the path of a proposed industrial park.

Ivan said his father always wanted to build a pond on the family's homestead, but that dream never materialized. In the early 1980s, Ivan sold a section of his land to a corporation that plans to construct an industrial park. Eventually, this development will devour the site, forcing the removal of General Stannard's house. When last I saw Ivan, he was haying below Cobble Hill, his last remaining piece of land. "*This* is the land I want to pass on," he told me.

The Wisconsin Experience and the Landscape of War

Without hard evidence, I can only speculate as to why the Brown family left the comforts of home to face the rigors of life on the Wisconsin frontier. Nevertheless, in 1857, Jason and Sarah Brown and their six children — Sarah, fifteen; Charlotte, fourteen; Warrington, twelve; Henrietta, eleven; Lucas, three; and Almina, two — left Vermont to emigrate west. Abandoning the rocky soil of Vermont for the rich land of southern Wisconsin undoubtedly motivated their journey across America. The fact that in 1846 Sarah's brother, Loammi K. Stannard, had settled in Janesville may have been another reason for the move, for sharing adjacent land was the common immigration pattern for the Hallidays, Browns, and Stannards. Another possible factor for the move may have been related to the troubled economic times of the mid-1850s.[1]

Photographs, family stories, and a few archival records provide but slim clues to the lives and personalities of Jason and Sarah Brown. A portrait of Sarah Stannard Brown shows a woman with her mouth drawn tightly downward, a mirror of the life pioneer women were forced to face. Aunt

Jason Brown was killed on the first day of the first major battle of the Civil War. With gun in hand, Jason looks defiantly forward in this studio tintype. Courtesy of Millicent Remington Owen.

Anne Winters remembered her father, Warrington, telling her that when he cried after nearly severing his finger while chopping wood his mother told him to stop, "for boys must never cry."[2] A faded tintype of Jason in his Civil War uniform matches the physical description given in his army records: hazel eyes, black hair, a dark complexion, and height 5′ 6″.[3]

When war broke out in 1861, the Brown family was living six miles west of Janesville, somewhere near the tiny village of Center, Wisconsin. Although warranty deeds, assessor's records, plat books, and censuses yield no references to the family, one city directory provides a possible clue to the fortunes of Jason and Sarah during their first year in Wisconsin. According to the directory, a Sarah Brown, boarding on West Milwaukee Street, worked in Janesville as a book folder, and a saloon worker at Milwaukee near River Street is named Jason Brown.[4] If, indeed, these people are my great-grandparents, I speculate that they may have worked in town in an attempt to save enough money to buy land and begin farming.

Although they may have planned to buy their own farm, that dream came to a tragic end in 1861. In May, Jason, age forty-two, drove his wagon into Janesville to enlist for three years in the Union Army.[5] Driven by a sense of duty and perhaps motivated by the need for steady work as well as the thrill of adventure, Jason joined other neighboring farmers and tradesmen to form Company D, Second Regiment, Wisconsin Volunteers. Along with nine other companies of the Wisconsin Second Brigade, the Janesville Volunteers trained for a month at Fort Randall in Madison. That June, Jason and 1,047 other Wisconsin volunteers made the long journey east by train. After exuberant greetings from citizens in Chicago, Toledo, and Cleveland, the volunteers, weaponless and wearing gray uniforms, arrived in Washington, D.C.[6]

Initially, the Second Brigade was assigned to Col. William T. Sherman's brigade and given an additional three weeks' training at Fort Corcoran, Virginia. On July 16, the brigade joined Union troops who were moving toward Confederate territory. On July 21, the opening day of the Battle of Bull Run, the inadequately trained Wisconsin Second, still dressed in gray, was the first regiment Sherman sent forward to engage the enemy line.[7]

The center of action on that first afternoon was a gentle slope southwest of Bull Run Creek known as Henry Hill. At the top of the hill stood a house occupied by an eighty-five-year-old invalid widow, Judith Carter Henry, and her family. Although ill and bedridden, Mrs. Henry refused to

seek shelter distant from the battle. Twice that day, her sons forcibly removed her from the house until she convinced them that she wished to
die in her own bed. At one point, Confederate sharpshooters placed themselves inside and around the house, making it the target for Union gunfire.
Artillery fire shattered Mrs. Henry's bed, wounding her in the neck and
side and almost blowing off one of her feet. Later that afternoon, Judith
Henry died.[8]

When Colonel Sherman gave the order for the Wisconsin Second to
strike at Henry Hill, Union troops standing behind the regiment saw their
gray uniforms and opened fire. After officers finally restored order, the
Second once again moved forward against the hill while firing upon units
from Virginia and South Carolina. At this point, someone in the Second
Regiment mistakenly thought he saw a Union flag among these units and
shouted: "You are shooting your friends! Stop, for God's sake! Spare your
own brothers." According to historian John Hennessey, "The firing slack-
ened and then exploded once more as the Confederates laced the Union
line with lead."[9] Divided into two wings, the demoralized and disorga-
nized Second Regiment was now incapable of seizing the initiative to take
Henry Hill. When Sherman ordered the Wisconsin troops to fall back to
re-form, two New York regiments mistook them for Confederates and
opened fire. This final tragic incident effectively paralyzed the unfortunate
Wisconsin Second.[10]

According to Bull Run's national park historian Alan Libby, most accounts of the battle argue that the Wisconsin Second's 15 percent loss was
largely due to the men wearing gray. "Those men died from friendly fire,"
Libby told me.[11]

During one of the attempts to take Henry Hill, Jason Brown fell, one of
three men killed in Company D.[12] Back home in Wisconsin, Sarah Brown
was now a widow; her oldest son, Warrington, sixteen, too young to enlist,
was forced to help support his mother, brother, and sisters. Three years
later, two months before he turned nineteen, Warrington would follow his
father's path and join the Union army.

On a silent, humid summer day, while visiting Bull Run, I imagined
the sweaty, wool-uniformed soldiers ascending the slope toward Judith
Henry's house. The blighted landscape shown in the postbattle photographs now has a gently undulating, grass-covered surface. A heavy blue
overcast hangs above the distant wooded hills, where bird sounds and the

smell of rich vegetation fill the air. Wildflowers frame the ridge leading to Henry House. Where Jason's comrades fell, mown grass covers the hidden graves on Bull Run's bloody field.

Prior to Jason's death, other people whose lives were intertwined with the Brown family had settled within a twelve-mile radius of Center. John and Anne Halliday and their children, Mary, twelve, William, ten, and an infant, John Francis, lived in nearby Tiffany. Sarah Brown's brother, Loammi Stannard, and his wife, Almira, lived two miles east of Center in Janesville township. My search for land belonging to the Brown and Halliday families turned up but one deed citation — a section of land belonging to Jason Brown's son-in-law, one Joshua Crall.[13] Frustrated by my lack of luck, I began driving around the countryside hoping to locate farms that still retained their nineteenth-century appearance. While much of the landscape was dotted with trailer homes and metal buildings, the extraordinarily well preserved Loammi Stannard farm stood out from among its neighbors. According to deeds, Stannard purchased land in 1846 and before his death in 1883 erected the house and cattle barn still found in 1995. According to the abstract, eight years after Almira's death in 1887, her daughter sold the farm for $12,000 to Richard Stark, a second-generation German immigrant.

When I drove up to the farm, I was greeted by Richard's son, Harry Stark, seventy-seven, and his sisters, Selma, eighty, and Martha, eighty-three, all of whom had been born on the Stannard farm. Harry took over the farm after his father's death in 1948, and Selma and Martha had worked for forty years at the Parker Pen Company in Janesville. Harry told me that local people have always referred to the farm as the Standard [*sic*] place. He thought that Loammi Stannard had built the house in 1853 and said the only change was the kitchen and combination woodshed/mudroom that his father added in the 1930s.

I spent two exciting days (and several short visits over the following years) studying the Stannard-Stark farm as a living artifact from a rapidly disappearing way of life in rural Wisconsin. Because few physical changes had apparently taken place since Almira Stannard's death, I was able to see the farm as it must have appeared to my pioneer ancestors. I also sensed that the Starks had made few changes, either in the farm's outward appearance or in their own lifestyle, since their father's death. I felt, there-

Except for the modern siding, the Stannard-Stark farmhouse remains relatively unchanged from its mid-nineteenth-century appearance. The Stannards lived on the farm from 1846 to 1895.

fore, that the farm and its occupants were truly locked into an earlier time period.

The outward symbols of the farm's continuity are the well-preserved buildings built between 1850 and 1940, including the Greek Revival farmhouse with its band-sawn scalloped window moldings. Although the original shutters have been removed and the walls unsympathetically re-sided, the moldings and porch trim still reveal the beauty of the original facade. The T-shaped interior contains three distinct living areas. The upright (west) wing has a bedroom and a sitting room which the Starks shut up in winter and use for entertaining the rest of the year. The center bay has a spacious dining room, a kitchen, and a mudroom/woodshed. The Starks call the dining room the "room of doors" because openings connect it to every room downstairs. The east bay has a combination sewing room and office, a bathroom, and a pantry with a small root cellar beneath.

The farm site also boasts a fine post-and-beam, board-and-batten cattle barn built ca. 1860. Its complex bracing system, constructed of white oak and walnut, reveals a high degree of craftsmanship. Like the house, this structure (now used as a machine shed) was in excellent condition in 1995.

Other buildings include a ca. 1883 board-and-batten barn, two smaller post-1900 outbuildings, and a milk house (now used as a pump house) from the 1930s. An alley of beautiful white maple trees, undoubtedly planted by the Stannards, stands between County Road A and the Starks' front door.

The village of Center lies about two miles west of the Stannard-Stark farm. Today, this quiet hamlet consists of a town hall, a remodeled church, and a cemetery. To the south, the surrounding landscape is dominated by a line of hills. The last time I visited the Stark family, the sky above Center was filled with dark clouds, promising rain. Watching the skyline, I thought about my Wisconsin pioneer family with their griefs and laborious daily tasks. How exhilarating it must have been at day's end to watch the horizon and dream of even better farmland to the west.

7

The Stannards of Taylors Falls, Minnesota

Lucas Kingsbury Stannard, Sarah Stannard's youngest brother, also left Vermont to farm in the West, where he became one of Minnesota's earliest settlers. The Stannard farm near Taylors Falls stands today in nearly pristine condition, a symbol of the Stannard family's worldly success.

Lucas Stannard was born in Georgia, Franklin County, Vermont, July 6, 1825.[1] As a child, he worked on the family farm until, at age seventeen, he became a teacher. According to his biographers, Stannard "early learned the art of raising corn, and the various cereals which grow on the Green Mountains; [he] fitted himself by means of the district school and application to the text-books in the chimney-corner."[2] When he was twenty-one, Stannard entered Vermont's Bakersfield Academy, where he studied the classics. After graduating with honors, he read law for three years in the office of Benjamin H. Smalley and Asa Owen Aldis in St. Albans while supporting himself by teaching during the winter season. After admission to the bar in 1850, Lucas emigrated west, where he drove a herd of cattle from St. Louis to Taylors Falls.[3] In 1858, Stannard married Harriet Stevenson, the niece of W. H. C. Folsom, a well-known Minnesota pioneer and historian. Born in Maine and educated at Northfield Seminary, New Hampshire, Harriet had moved west, where she became a teacher in the first school in Chisago County, Minnesota.[4]

Using his education, ambition, and adherence to the work ethic, Stannard made a name for himself in the rapidly growing village as the first county attorney and, at various times, a prosecuting attorney, a probate judge, and a county surveyor. After terminating a partnership, Stannard practiced alone for a number of years and later formed what one biographer called an "unfortunate" five-year partnership in the logging and lumbering business. An eleven-year partnership in general merchandise and lumbering proved more successful. In retirement, Stannard continued his law practice and worked in real estate.[5]

Stannard was also deeply involved in state politics. In 1856, he helped organize the county's first Republican club. The following year he was elected county delegate to the Minnesota Constitutional Convention, where he helped write the first state constitution. He was also the nominee for secretary of state on the first Republican ticket.[6] In 1859, Stannard was elected state senator from Pine and Chisago Counties. As a legislator, he sponsored a successful bill to tax railroads on gross earnings. According to biographer E. V. Smalley, the bill "was the most just and equitable system of taxation ever adopted for compelling railroad companies to bear the share of the burden of the state's taxation."[7] In 1884, President Arthur appointed Stannard registrar of the land office in Taylors Falls, a position he held until the end of Grover Cleveland's first administration in 1889. During his long career, Stannard also served as mayor, trustee, village attorney, and president of the board of education.[8]

Very little information about the private character of Luke Stannard or the lives of family members is included in the standard biographies. A few scattered family stories help to fill in this gap. According to one story, Stannard paid a substitute to serve in his place during the Civil War, and the unfortunate soldier died in battle and is buried in Taylors Falls.[9] According to another story, Lucas and Harriet Stannard were described as combining the stoical qualities of their New England heritage with the aspirations of the upper middle class. Harriet Stannard, according to this source, was a "stern and private woman" and so old-fashioned and frugal that she hauled water on a shoulder yoke and wore outdated clothing. Although she was careful with money, Harriet insisted on having her own furniture shipped from Vermont to Stillwater, where Lucas had to move it to Taylors Falls by oxcart.[10]

The Stannard houses and farms reflect their owners' wealth and social aspirations. In architectural terms, the Stannard farm in Taylors Falls, like the family farms in Vermont and Wisconsin, stands at the elite end of the vernacular scale. The New England and midwestern houses and farms continue to be used today because the Stannards could afford superior materials and demand a high level of craftsmanship.

The design of the Stannard farmhouse in Taylors Falls combines elite stylistic elements from the Greek Revival and Victorian periods. The original house, now the east bay, was built in 1854 as an upright temple with a broad, gabled roof and a Federal doorway — a mirror of Lucas and Harriet Stannard's New England heritage. According to Kaye Grossmann, the present owner, Stannard chose a builder from back east to design his house because no one in Taylors Falls could meet Stannard's high standards.[11]

In 1891, the adjoining Victorian turret bays were added to provide space for Lucas's newly married son, Luke, and his wife, Lottie. Adding the twin-turret wing increased the total number of rooms to eighteen, with nine additional closets. The house now had three front rooms, including a library with space for twelve hundred volumes in the east bay, and a parlor and sitting room in the new twin-turret bays. The local newspaper described the house as "by far the finest residence in this section of Minnesota."[12]

The Stannard farmhouse has passed through many transitions. While the exterior of the 1854 bay retains most of its original appearance, the Stannards and later residents made many interior changes. In an attempt to modernize the interior, Lottie Stannard removed and discarded the marble shelves that once lined the library walls. Prior to the Grossmann purchase in 1977, the house had been used for several years as rental property, and at the end of that period there was talk of burning it down. Over

The Stannard farmhouse retains much of its original character. The three-bay composition includes the 1854 Greek Revival bay (left), the 1891 turret bays (center), and a modern remodeling of the carriage shelter (right).

the past nineteen years, the Grossmanns have been slowly working toward total renovation.

The Grossmanns are also gradually renovating the 1891 addition. A wall that once separated the parlor and the living room was removed prior to their occupancy, but the original pine floors and areas of period woodwork remain. A narrow, hall-like room near the rear entrance once housed two cookstoves on which food was prepared during the harvest season. Behind the west turret is another small room where Lucas spent his final years. An unusual "hidden room" is enclosed beneath the staircase.

To house their Kentucky shorthorn cattle, the Stannards built an English-style bank barn in 1891. Like the house, the barn is an architectural showpiece. In terms of style, craftsmanship, aesthetics, and present state of preservation, only the Loammi K. Stannard barn in Janesville, Wisconsin, rivals this fine vernacular structure. Especially pleasing is the barn's interior. The pegged round-log-beam and hewn-post framework is as plumb as the day the barn was raised. The roof is supported by an elaborate system of hewn rafters and struts. While the textures of rough planking and raw stone are especially pleasing, the barn's volume is its chief merit, for, upon entering, the eye is drawn outward and upward to the structure's cathedrallike ceiling.

The folk culture of the Stannard farm has an interesting twist. When I interviewed Kaye Grossmann, she told me that she feels a special rapport with the farmhouse. The house is "in her family's blood," she told me, and her two children feel "as if they had been born in the house." Ms. Grossmann firmly believes that the Stannard house is haunted because their dog often barks at the west bedroom's open door but refuses to enter the room.[13]

Lucas Stannard's success did not extend into the following generations. In the case of Lucas's son, Luke Stannard, and Luke's son, Conway Stannard, early success ended in public humiliation. Luke Stannard was born in Taylors Falls in 1859. When he was seven, Luke and his father drove a herd of shorthorn cattle from Louisville, Kentucky, to Taylors Falls. When he was a young man, Luke spent three terms at the Preparatory School of Carleton College, Northfield, Minnesota, but soon left college to return home to join his father in the cattle business. Later, Luke, like his father, was active in community affairs, serving as a county commissioner, a school board member, and a member of the village council.[14]

In 1909, Luke organized the Stannard State Bank in Taylors Falls. This successful enterprise ended in 1933, when, due in part to the Depression, the bank failed. According to family stories, Luke and his partner, his son, Conway, were "whipped men" after the bank failure, and both felt "absolutely devastated" when townspeople ignored them.[15] According to another story, Luke had once told Conway that the Depression would never affect the bank, but when Luke came home one noon to inform the family that the bank had failed that morning, he had shaved off his mustache, apparently in an odd attempt to hide his identity from townspeople!

In the aftermath of the bank's closing, Luke was forced to sell family land holdings in order to reimburse depositors, but Conway saved the farm by personally assuming a $10,000 mortgage. Years later, Ruth Stannard, Conway's wife, recalled that after the bank closed, her husband often went down to the pasture to sit and think and to escape the eyes of the town. During the 1930s and 1940s, Luke continued to live on the farm, where he supported himself by small farming, gardening, and rent from apartments he owned.[16] In time, many Taylors Falls citizens came to forgive Luke Stannard. On his eightieth birthday, the local newspaper noted in a laudatory article that Luke always arose at 5 A.M. and, accompanied by his shepherd dog, rounded up his herd for the morning milking.[17]

The Hallidays, Hollidays, and Browns of Goodhue County, Minnesota

The Mississippi River near Lake City, Minnesota, broadens widely to form Lake Pepin, one of the most beautiful river-lakes in America. As early as 1767, the English explorer Jonathan Carver described the beauty of the landscape surrounding the river valley near Lake Pepin: "Came to the great medows or plains. I found excellent good land and very pleasant country. One might travel all day and only see now and then a small pleasant groves of oak and walnut. This country is covered with grass which affords excellent pasturage for the buffeloe which here are very plenty."[1] When Minnesota became a territory in 1849, these rich lands west of the Mississippi were opened for immigrant settlement. Land seekers arriving by steamer from points south disembarked at Lake City or its neighboring village, Red Wing, eleven miles upstream, to settle in the area.

In 1860, as part of this pioneer movement, John and Anne Halliday and their three children, William, Mary, and John Francis, moved from Wisconsin to the bluff country of Florence township, Goodhue County, high above the river valley near Lake City, Minnesota. Soon after their arrival,

Anne gave birth to her last child, Ellsworth. Five years later, the Hallidays' Wisconsin neighbors, Warrington Brown, twenty, his widowed mother, Sarah, fifty, his brother, Luke, sixteen, and his sister, Almina, fifteen, arrived from Center, Wisconsin, to settle in a new home near the Hallidays' Florence township farmstead.[2]

During the past several years I have made many journeys to the bluff country of Florence township, where, initially, I found three farm sites that once belonged to the Hallidays and Browns. Following the contour of an early dirt trail, a winding gravel road ascends to a plateau about a mile above the river. As I drive along, I try to imagine early settlers climbing the hill by wagon after leaving the dock below. The landscape along the river and the farmland high above it seem relatively unchanged from that era. On the sides of the road, yellow sandstone and gray limestone outcrops — soft, shaley stone that settlers used for house and barn foundations — jut from the banks carved by the first road builders. An untended cemetery, its moss-covered stones overgrown with scrub vegetation, stands at the turn of the road. At the top of the hill, West Florence Ridge overlooks Gilbert Valley in adjacent Wabasha County. On that ridge, along Sugar Loaf Creek in sections 32 and 33, lie the farm sites that once belonged to Warrington Brown, John and Anne Halliday, and William and Marilla Hancock Holliday. (William Holliday and his descendants spell their name with an *o*.)[3]

Visiting Florence township today is a poignant experience for me, although since it was first settled many changes have taken place along West Florence Ridge. A three-story Victorian farmhouse, built after the Hallidays left the township, stands on my great-grandparents' farm site. One mile west are the ruins of the William and Marilla Holliday farm, and a cornfield fills the space where Warrington and Mary Brown's farmhouse once stood. Although the original buildings are gone, the landscape, so reminiscent of that found in Scotland and England, still evokes for me a sense of what my ancestors must once have felt when they first ascended Florence Ridge.

Hazel Wimmer, a widow in her eighties, and her sons, John and Lee, own the Halliday farm site today. The original farmhouse was razed in 1916, when Hazel's father built a large Victorian house for his family. Hazel Wimmer showed me a 1909 family photograph of a two-room, L-shaped house that undoubtedly belonged to John and Anne Halliday.

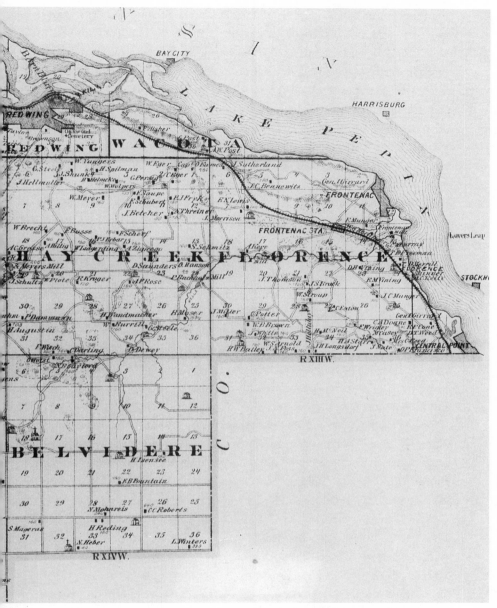

*Lands deeded to John Halliday and Warrington Brown are shown in Andreas's 1874
Minnesota atlas, Goodhue County plat map, 93. (See Florence township farmsites marked
"J. Halliday," section 33, and "W. B. Brown," section 32.) Only those people who agreed in
advance to purchase the atlas had their property identified. This may account for the absence
of William Holliday's name in section 33.*

Standing features that date to the Halliday era include an 1881, hand-crafted post-and-beam barn, built a year before the Hallidays moved to North Dakota, and the huge oaks that frame the farm's driveway.

William and Marilla Holliday homesteaded a mile west of William's parents' farm. Marilla was the daughter of Joseph Woods Hancock, a prominent missionary who was also the first white settler in Goodhue County. Born in Orford, New Hampshire, Joseph emigrated in 1849 from Saratoga Springs, New York, to Red Wing, Minnesota Territory, where he became a teacher among the Dakota and an organizer of the local Presbyterian church. Joseph's wife, Martha Maria Houghton, a sister of Henry Houghton, the Boston publisher, gave birth to Marilla, their only child, in 1848 and died in 1851, leaving the three-year-old Marilla in her father's care.[4]

Between 1864 and 1872, Hancock preached and farmed in the West Florence area. Entries from Hancock's diary contain the only record of the lives of John Halliday, William Holliday, and Warrington Brown during the time they lived in Goodhue County. Hancock's references to his own farm help us to understand common building practices among settlers along Florence Ridge. Hancock wrote that after purchasing land a mile east of John Halliday, he bought nails and lumber in Frontenac, hauled stone from nearby deposits, and with the help of neighbors raised a barn and built a summer kitchen.[5]

In 1864, Hancock became the first pastor of the West Florence Presbyterian Church. After meeting for several years in a log structure, the congregation constructed a frame building in 1871 where John Halliday was a church elder. In this building Mary Halliday and Warrington Brown and William Holliday and Marilla Hancock met and began their courtships.[6]

After they married in 1875, William and Marilla Holliday purchased land and built a farm which a lifelong resident of the area, William Witt, has called "a local showplace."[7] Like the Halliday site, William and Marilla's farm sits on a gentle slope overlooking Gilbert Valley. A 1928 photograph shows the appearance of the farm before demolition began in the 1980s. All that remains of the original farm are the house walls, the barn foundation, the stone walls of the chicken coop, and two huge oaks and a cottonwood that stand in front of the farmhouse door. Originally, the farm had a T-shaped frame farmhouse, an English barn, and several smaller buildings, including the fieldstone chicken coop. My study of the ruins of the farm shows that the house had a parlor, a living/dining room, a kitchen, an add-on summer kitchen, two enclosed porches, and two upstairs bedrooms. The parlor appears to have been unheated, while the adjoining living/dining room had a stove or heater. Mr. Witt thought that the house was built in the 1850s, with the canopy porch and the larger open porch added in the 1880s. Such features as the Queen Anne-inspired porch columns, fish-scale shingles, relief figures on the front door, and interior decorative moldings definitely postdate the 1850s.

The Holliday barn (only the foundation stands today) was an English barn, a style still found in diminishing numbers in southeastern Minnesota. A typical English barn in this region has a sandstone foundation, vertical-plank red or white siding, and a cupola or ventilator in the center of the ridgeline. Remnants of the Holliday barn show that it had a pink-sandstone foundation and tongue-and-groove siding.[8]

When I walked diagonally one mile northwest of the Holliday farm, I climbed a hill to the site of my grandfather Warrington Brown's farm. A dot in the northwest corner of section 32 on the 1874 Andreas map pinpoints where the farmhouse stood. Mr. Witt told me that while plowing he occasionally turns up a foundation stone, ostensibly from my grandfather's farm. Mr. Witt's brother-in-law, Mr. Buck, remembers a square, wooden-sided granary on the site that may have been my grandfather's. Because the buildings stood on high ground, both men think that the farm at one time must have had a windbreak. When I see this landscape I think of the following quote from Wright Morris: "In all my life I've never seen in anything so crowded, so full of something, as the rooms of a vacant house. Sometimes I think only vacant houses are occupied."[9] If a landscape can be thought of as "vacant," Morris's observation mirrors my feelings about the windswept cornfield atop Florence Ridge, the land where my grandparents made their first home.

In 1996, 118 years after my grandparents left Goodhue County, I learned that Northern States Power Company plans to store highly radioactive spent fuel from its Prairie Island nuclear plant in Red Wing at three sites along the bluffs in Florence township. This proposed thirty-million-dollar project, approved by the Minnesota legislature and slated for completion by 1999, has been challenged by a group of citizens who represent fifteen hundred residents in the township. The present environmental profile of

The William and Marilla Holliday farm was a model example of a regional type of architecture common to Goodhue County during the period 1870 to 1914. Progress, recession, and neglect have all but eliminated landmark farms from the southeastern Minnesota landscape.

Florence township is described in a newspaper article as follows: "The township contains a mixture of riverfront woods and plateaus of farm fields that give way to steep bluffs. Besides clusters of people near Hwy. 61 in Frontenac and in Old Frontenac, a historic village on the river, the area contains a golf course, marina, wetlands, and Frontenac State Park, which last year attracted 91,000 visitors." [10]

Should this project succeed, the lives of those who live on the ridge and the pristine landscape they inhabit will be changed forever.

The Browns of Pipestone County, Minnesota

Driving to Pipestone on a May afternoon, I see massive cumulus clouds lazily floating in a bright blue sky. Black, loamy fields have been recently seeded after two weeks of hard rain. The vista is broken by sporadic tree clumps, planted by pioneer farmers to break the fierce winter winds. On this rolling sea the clumps resemble ships anchored in a great harbor. This spring, the smells and sounds are rich and varied. The scents of freshly applied tar and new-mown grass arise from the road and ditches. Red-winged blackbirds cling to tall strands of grass, where the wind swings them precariously. Meadowlarks sing, and hawks circle overhead. Mallards rest in ponds and mudholes. Farm families have picked the fields clean of rocks and piled them neatly like crude pyramids at the ends of field rows. Along the road stand aging wooden telephone poles towered over by highlines — mute giants whose extended arms delicately grasp the lines that run from horizon to horizon.

When I make the same drive in late summer, a heavy haze of heat and moisture fills the sky. The landscape is a giant green-and-brown patchwork quilt dulled by the sun. Bright yellow black-eyed susans provide the only color on this preautumnal prairie. Harvest-ready corn, tasseled and dry, stands in the windless fields.

In November, the prairie sights and sounds are frozen beneath the snowbanks. A period of "unseasonable" warmth has set in after a week of minus-twenty-five-degree-wind-chill temperatures. A recent heavy snow has blown into drifts and hardened into snowdunes that resemble giant lumps of frosting, their rippled surfaces made shiny by the driving wind. As I drive toward the prairie, the pale blue sky is filled with thin wisps of white clouds blown into silky strands by the winter wind. As the sun moves to the southwest, the clouds are suddenly rimmed pink. Today, the windbreaks look like lonely islands rather than bobbing ships. The naked tree clumps are a dark brown, their delicate branches etched against the pale sky. Human-made objects — barns, telephone poles, and railroad signs — seem stark and lonely against the blinding whiteness. The only movement in this silent landscape is a crow that alights along the roadside in search of stray bits of grain. As the car approaches, it flies off and lands in a nearby field.

The most prominent geographical feature on this landscape is the two-thousand-foot plateau that runs from the northeast corner of South Dakota to the Blue Earth River in northwest Iowa. French explorers called this formation the Coteau des Prairies (Highland of the Prairies). To a contemporary traveler on Highway 23, the Coteau first appears near Green Valley, Lyon County, where it stretches like a dark blue ribbon across the western horizon. Near the village of Ruthton in Pipestone County, the Coteau rises dramatically to form the rolling hills of Buffalo Ridge.

According to geologists George M. Schwartz and George A. Thiel, the Coteau is a large plateau or massive ridge that "extends southeastward from the headwaters of the Big Sioux River in South Dakota, across southwestern Minnesota, and into Iowa, where it forms the divide between the Missouri and Mississippi drainage basins." The geologists further describe this formation as "smoothly undulating or rolling . . . with two terminal moraine zones that are irregularly broken by steep hills, knolls, and small ridges. The south ends of these moraines rest on ridges

"Hole-in-the-Mountain," a slice of virgin prairie in the Coteau region of Lincoln County, is a microcosm of living things: bluestem, pasque flowers, false foxglove, brome grass, purple prairie clover, and yarrow, among other species. The area is protected by the Nature Conservancy.

of the old Sioux Quartzite, a metamorphic rock that dates from the Proterozoic era . . . which is exposed at various places in Pipestone, Rock, and Yellow Medicine counties."[1]

George Catlin and Joseph N. Nicollet, the first explorers to reach what would later become southwestern Minnesota, were rhapsodic in their descriptions of the Coteau. After visiting the region in 1836, Catlin, artist, writer, and scholar of Indian life, recorded this description of the Coteau:

> There is a sublime grandeur in (the) things . . . here, which must be seen and felt to be understood. . . . There is a majesty in (this) ground . . . that inspires us with awe and reverence. / (A person would have to) . . . have the soul of a brute . . . who could gallop his horse . . . over these swells and terraces of green that rise continually ahead . . . without feeling awe and admiration . . . / when he rises to (the top of) the last terrace . . . one's . . . body and mind both seem to have entered a new element . . . /

(The body feels) . . . as free as the very wind it inhales, The (mind) . . . as expanded and infinite as the boundless imagery that is spread in the distance around him. / Such is the *Coteau du prairie*.[2]

At the place where the Coteau enters southwestern Minnesota lies the site of the Pipestone Quarry. Plains Indians believe the Spirit formed their people from the quarry's red stone, and they revere the site as sacred. For centuries, Plains tribes have gathered here to solemnize intertribal treaties and to quarry the red stone, which is used to sculpt calumets (peace pipes) and other ceremonial totems.

In 1836, Catlin arrived at the quarry accompanied by an English traveler, Robert Serril Wood, and a native guide, O-kup-kee. Catlin's party had been detained by a band of Santee Sioux near Traverse des Sioux, 150 miles from the quarry, and warned not to trespass on the sacred ground. A warrior told Catlin, "No white man has been to the red pipe and none shall go. You see that this pipe is a part of our flesh. The red men are a part of the red stone. If the white men take away a piece of the red pipe stone, it is a hole made in our flesh, and the blood will always run. We cannot stop the blood from running."[3] In spite of warnings, Catlin's party pressed on to the quarry, where they found a band of Dakotas who allowed the artist time to paint scenes of native life. Catlin's drawings, paintings, and writings provide us with the first on-site documentation of the quarry as a geological feature, a source of myth, and a place sacred to the natives of the Plains. Art historian Rena N. Coen argues that Catlin's work stands as "one of the first to study Indian cultures from a serious ethnological point of view and not merely as quaint curiosities in a wild and savage land."[4]

During his visit Catlin heard the Dakota myth of creation and its connection to the red stone:

That in the time of a great freshet, which took place many centuries ago, and destroyed all the nations of the earth, all the tribes of the red men assembled on the *Coteau du Prairie*, to get out of the way of the waters. After they had all gathered here from all parts, the water continued to rise, until at length it covered them all in a mass, and their flesh was converted into red pipe stone. Therefore, it has always been considered neutral ground — it belonged to all tribes alike, and all were allowed to get it and smoke it together. While they were all drowning in a mass,

George Catlin's Pipestone Quarry on the Coteau des Prairies, *1836–1837. National Museum of American Art, Smithsonian Institution, gift of Mrs. Joseph Harrison, Jr.*

a young woman, K-wap-tah-w (a virgin) caught hold of the foot of a very large bird that was flying over, and was carried to the top of a high cliff . . . Here she had twins, and their father was the war-eagle, and her children have since peopled the earth.[5]

In the summer of 1838, Joseph N. Nicollet visited the Coteau while exploring the vast region now comprising the eastern Dakotas, Minnesota, and Iowa. According to his biographers, Edmund Bray and Martha Bray, Nicollet, like Catlin before him, was enthralled with the prairie landscape. In Nicollet's report, "the appearance of this landscape takes precedence over the narrative and becomes the central theme," the Brays argue.[6] The opening of the report captures the unusual nature of the virgin prairie as Nicollet viewed it:

It is neither a mountainous, nor a hilly, nor an absolutely flat country; exhibiting undulations of the surface that are not entitled to these usual appellations. There are hillocks, swells, and uplands; but they have a longitudinal and horizontal, rather than a vertical projection. In other words, it is a beautiful arrangement of upland and lowland plains; that give it an aspect *sui generis.*[7]

Nicollet's account of his arrival at the Pipestone Quarry during the summer of 1838 shows how deeply he was influenced by the myths surrounding the sacred site. Natives had told him the quarry

> was opened by the great spirit of thunder, and one cannot visit it without being greeted by the rumblings and the lightning and storms that accompany them . . . We were not ½ mile from the valley of thunder when lightning and heavy rain burst upon us and violent winds nearly upset Mr. Renville's wagon, holding us up for several minutes before we were able to begin the short descent into the valley.[8]

In spite of its incomparable beauty and sacred character, early contacts at the quarry sometimes included violence. In February 1857, a band of outlaw Sioux, led by Inkpaduta, killed fifty-five settlers near Spirit Lake, Iowa. Inkpaduta's band captured four settlers, Abbie Gardner, Margaret Marble, Lydia Noble, and Elizabeth Thatcher, and for six weeks marched them across the prairie into Minnesota and the Dakotas. In April, the captives spent one day at the quarry while their captors carved pipes.

Abbie, who had lost her parents, a brother, a sister, a niece, and a nephew to the marauders at Spirit Lake, later wrote a history in which she described the quarry, recorded native legends, and noted the area's influence upon Henry Wadsworth Longfellow's *Hiawatha*. Although she was under extreme duress as a captive, Abbie could still recall the beauty of the Coteau nearly thirty years later:

> The natural scenery along the Big Sioux is grand and beautiful. From the summit of the bluffs, the eye can view thousands of acres of richest vale and undulating prairie; while through it, winding along like a monstrous serpent, is the river, its banks fringed with maple, oak and elm. Had we been in a mood to appreciate it, we surely should have enjoyed this beautiful picture.[9]

A year after Gardner's capture, a treaty with the Yankton branch of the Sioux nation secured the tribe's unrestricted right to quarry the red stone, a treaty that has been consistently honored since 1870. When homesteaders began moving into southwestern Minnesota prior to the Civil War, the population of surrounding counties grew steadily through the 1860s and 1870s, while fear of conflict kept settlers away from claims immediately adjacent to the sacred quarry. The slow growth of Pipestone County is reflected in the absence of names in the 1860 federal census and the tardy completion in 1871 of a decade-old plan to survey the county. A year after finishing the survey, one square mile around the quarry was set aside as a reservation.[10]

A trickle of white settlement began in the fall of 1873, when Charles H. Bennett, a pharmacist from LeMars, Iowa, his family, and a group of friends crossed the prairie and camped near the quarry. As a result of this visit, Bennett decided to plat a town site about a mile west of the reservation. A Rock Rapids, Iowa, group — D. C. Whitehead, Daniel E. Sweet, Job Whitehead, and J. F. Eckleston — visited the quarry the following spring and decided to locate on Bennett's town site. Daniel Sweet surveyed the township named in his honor. Soon after, Bennett and his brother O. W. Bennett, the Whiteheads, Sweet, and John Lowry began hauling oxcart loads of lumber for claim shanties from Luverne, twenty-four miles away. Claims filed by this group led to the formation of Pipestone City.[11]

During these early settlement years, the connection between the homesteaders and their environment differed markedly from the relationship to nature experienced by natives and explorers. The writings of O. E. Rölvaag and the reminiscences recorded by prairie settlers reveal that while the early homesteaders were often entranced by the beauty of the landscape, loneliness and natural disasters often tempered the prairie experience.

In O. E. Rölvaag's *Giants in the Earth*, Per Hansa's family crosses the prairie of southern Minnesota from Fillmore County to Dakota Territory in 1873. As they approach the Coteau, Rölvaag tells us that "out on the sky line the huge plain now began to swell and rise, almost as if an abscess were forming under the skin of the earth. Although this elevation lay somewhat out of his course, Per Hansa swung over and held straight toward the highest part of it."[12] Although the Norwegian immigrant in this novel is both fearful of and drawn to this landscape, as the sun begins to sink his mood changes to despondency: "suddenly the landscape had grown desolate; something bleak and cold had come into the silence, filling it with terror. . . . Behind them, along the way they had come, the plain lay dark green and lifeless, under the gathering shadow of the dim, purple sky."[13]

For Beret, Per Hansa's wife, life on the prairie was difficult from the beginning. Although Beret seemed to be enchanted with the prairie because of its resemblance to the sea, she soon sensed a "difference," for "this formless prairie had no heart that beat, no waves that sang, no soul that could be touched."[14] The absence of bird and insect sounds, the lack of growing things, the isolation from neighbors, and, more importantly, the great silence of prairie space ultimately produced Beret's acute depression. Beret's thoughts reveal the alienation she felt in this unfamiliar environment: "Had they travelled into some nameless, abandoned region? Could no living thing exist out here, in the empty, desolate, endless wastes of green and blue? . . . How *could* existence go on, she thought, desperately? If life is to thrive and endure, it must at least have something to hide behind!"[15]

The experience of the homesteader who arrived in Pipestone County in the 1870s was similar to that shared by the characters in Rölvaag's novel. In 1894, Charles Bennett wrote that while the early settlers were "in search of a beautiful place to dwell [they also found] a rough and wild wilderness and their settlement was attended with hardships, trials, and tribulations sufficient to deter the most resolute."[16]

Biographies of Pipestone County pioneers gathered by Arthur Rose for his 1911 history echo these feelings. Christ Gilbertson, one of Rose's pioneers who, like Per Hansa, had emigrated from Fillmore County, recalled that when he first saw Pipestone County in 1894 it was a "raw, untempered prairie land."[17] In the absence of trees, Gilbertson and his family sought shelter for four years in a tiny, two-room sod house. Another pioneer, Robert M. Doughty, who arrived in 1879 by prairie schooner from Olmstead County, Minnesota, told Rose that his first shelter was a dugout covered with reeds, coarse grass, and hay. During the great blizzard of 1880–81, Doughty's dugout was buried in "mammoth snowdrifts" from which he had to carve steps to reach the outside world. Doughty burned twisted hay for fuel and ground wheat in a coffee mill for bread.[18]

My grandfather Warrington Brown waded armpit-deep through two streams while walking twenty miles from Flandreau, Dakota Territory, to Pipestone to file a claim for his brother, Luke Brown, in the early spring of 1879. When he arrived at Daniel Sweet's claim shack, he found it overflowing with land seekers. When he learned that the nearest hotel was in Luverne, Warrington insisted that he be allowed to stay in the shack overnight. Years later, he recalled that he caught a terrible cold after sleeping in wet clothes near a crack in the shack's door.[19]

Natural disasters were common during the settlement years. In August 1876, the sky suddenly blackened with grasshoppers, who rapidly destroyed the county's grain crops, gardens, young trees, and cuttings. Following the infestation, many settlers abandoned the region. When it appeared that no one would permanently settle in the county, Bennett decided to live on his claim until Christmas as a gesture to encourage settlement. When grasshoppers did not reappear, over one hundred claims were filed the following summer.[20]

Besides grasshoppers, fire, wind, and blizzards also made life difficult for the pioneers. Although ecologically essential, prairie fires made crop growing and shelter building hazardous. In October 1879, chimney sparks on the J. M. Chute claim dropped on dry grass. The *Pipestone County Star* reported that "in an instant the prairie was a sheet of flame, and in an hour's time the fire spread in an easterly direction for miles, and many of our people went out to the scene but were of course powerless to do anything. Mr. Chute lost his barn and was quite seriously burned himself."[21]

Wind and a rainstorm, accompanied by lightning, in the summer of 1879 killed four horses hitched to a wagon. The following year a rainstorm turned Pipestone's main street into what the local paper called a "first-class river." This storm also lifted the new school off its foundation and carried it some distance away. Paradoxically, violent weather was sometimes followed by a dramatic natural phenomenon that made prairie life visually pleasant. During the summer of the violent rainstorm, the *Star* described the following mirage:

At about 9 o'clock A.M. while the regions south and southeast were being visited by a brisk rainfall, and while a bank of cumulus clouds was lying a few degrees about the western horizon, the county for about 50 miles along the Big Sioux and in width about 25 miles seemed lifted in mid air, and lay spread out to view, with its farms and buildings, hills and valleys, and lights and shadows, in the most bewildering way.[22]

The winter of 1880–81, however, was treacherous. A blizzard that began in October 1880 was the worst calamity to hit the county during its early years. In intensity and duration, the winter that lasted from October

1880 until the end of April 1881 has never been surpassed. Rain that fell on October 14 turned to sleet and snow, and hurricane-force winds blew the snow into twenty-foot drifts the following day. After two months of plummeting temperatures, a five-day blizzard arrived on Christmas Day 1880. Week-long blizzards occurred regularly throughout January and February 1881. In January, schools closed for the winter after the temperature fell to thirty below. Two March blizzards carried the winter's heaviest snowfall, and additional blizzards and heavy snow arrived on five separate occasions between March 14 and April 11. On April 26, the first train since February 1 made its way into the village, ending eighty days of isolation from the outside world.[23]

The way homesteaders coped with the disastrous blizzard year has become part of the county's folklore. Rose records the story of Horace Gilmore's wife, who was snowbound with relatives in Luverne for nine weeks.[24] Another biography notes that when Gilbert Gilbertson and a neighbor were returning home on snowshoes pulling a hand-sled loaded with provisions purchased in Lake Benton nineteen miles away, they were suddenly enveloped in a blizzard a mile from their destination. After wandering aimlessly throughout the night, the men luckily stumbled upon a neighbor's claim shanty, a shelter from which they made their way safely home the following day. The unfortunate Gilbertson, however, froze both feet.[25]

My grandfather, too, remembered burning brooms, straw, hay, and flax for fuel that winter. In order to gather fuel at Woodstock, a village thirteen miles away, Warrington would wait until 3 A.M., when the snow crust was at its hardest, to drive his team of horses across the snow-packed Rock River. Warrington later recalled: "I had nothing to guide me but the stars; when the day dawned I was in sight of the village [of Woodstock]. I got three forths cord of wood for five dollars and started back before the sun would melt the crust. I arrived home about 10 [A.M.]."[26]

A handful of stories about my grandparents' pioneer experiences has been passed down through the years. Warrington, his wife, Mary, and their infant son, Paul, left Lake City for Pipestone County in the spring of 1878. According to a cherished family story, their first home was built of sod. When I was a child, my mother told me that the sod house stood at the northeast corner of Hiawatha and Centennial in downtown Pipestone, the site of Daniel Sweet's claim shanty.

The Warrington and Mary Brown homestead is a rare surviving example of a pioneer frame structure once commonly found on the prairie country of southwestern Minnesota. Influenced by the Colonial hall-and-parlor plan and the two-room log house, this Greek Revival structure reveals the upright temple form, door and window moldings, and pilasterlike corner boards.

Within a year of his arrival in Grange township, Grandfather had built a permanent family home, a frame structure that stands today. A most unusual feature rests beneath its clapboard siding: three walls of jasper quartzite fieldstone. The story of the origin of these walls is another treasured piece of family folklore. Grandfather told his grandson, Stan Morgan, that he built the walls, leaving openings where a rifle could be mounted, to protect his family from Indian attack.[27] Stan told me that when our grandfather hauled house lumber from Luverne by sleigh he wore a bearskin coat, covered his legs with a horsehide blanket, and periodically ran alongside his team.

My aunts had another version of this story. Once, while Grandfather was making his way home with a load of lumber, a sudden blizzard swept across the prairie. As he arrived near home, the only way he could locate his house was by the curling chimney smoke. When I was told this story as a child, I always imagined a man wrapped in a heavy coat, holding a whip, and walking beside a sleigh with wide wooden runners — a small dark figure silhouetted against a bleak white landscape.

As I drive through southwestern Minnesota in 1996, I realize that the landscape surrounding Pipestone remains relatively unchanged from the days when I lived there. Two-lane Highway 23 still winds through Buffalo Ridge near Ruthton until it becomes an eight-mile straight line between the village of Holland and Pipestone. The absence of billboards and the presence of wooden-post fences and glass-insulator telephone poles remind me that I am driving into a country that is still sparsely populated. Turning off Highway 23 onto a gravel road, I drive past my grandparents' farm and stop to enjoy the vista to the west. Although the natural beauty of southwestern Minnesota is more subtle than the bluff country along Florence Ridge, the prairie landscape is as enchanting to me as it must have been to my grandparents.

As I drive into Pipestone and down Main Street, I see the quartzite buildings that Scottish craftsmen erected in the 1880s. Before I drive down Third Avenue to the house where I was born, I first cut over to Fourth Avenue and drive past the house Grandfather Brown built after leaving the farm in 1891. Although the porch where Grandfather and I sat on summer afternoons is gone, I am once again reminded of the bond that made our relationship so wonderfully special.

North Dakota Pioneers:
The Hallidays, Hollidays, and Stramblads

One hundred years after my ancestors arrived in North Dakota, my sister Courtenay and I made two journeys there to search for places in Kidder and Barnes Counties where John and Anne Halliday and their descendants had settled. We knew that in 1881, the Hallidays and their children, John Francis, Ellsworth, William, and William's wife, Marilla, had sold their farms in Goodhue County, Minnesota, and moved to the newly opened farmland of North Dakota. Although John and Anne were in their sixties, they were willing, nevertheless, to sacrifice a familiar way of life to become pioneers once again. Their North Dakota experience reveals that confronting nature and accepting change were goals tantamount to improving their economic lot.

Courtenay and I found that North Dakota's drift prairie, where sky and land meet in all directions, could, over a two-year period, change dramatically. In 1985, as the result of a drought, small lakes were ghostly alkaline patches resembling buffalo bones; two years later, however, the same places were green, fertile, and teeming with wild birds.

At the outset of our first journey we knew very little about the Halli-days' North Dakota pioneer experience beyond a few dates and place-names. Prior to our second journey, I visited the National Archives in Washington, D.C., where I found John Francis Holliday's name in an early Kidder County plat book. While we were studying the plat map during our second trip, my sister recognized the name Stramblad on a section near John Francis Holliday's farm. In the 1930s, Courtenay had known the Stramblad family, and the plat book entry became a link to our North Dakota heritage.[1]

As North Dakota historian Elwyn B. Robinson points out, the 1880s was the period of the Great Dakota Boom: "In this decade occurred the most extensive railroad construction, the greatest immigration, the most expan-sion in manufacturing, and the fastest growth of cities that the nation has yet witnessed."[2]

At the time the Hallidays left Minnesota, the Northern Pacific Railroad was advertising in two hundred American and Canadian newspapers to at-tract settlers to Dakota Territory. During the year the Hallidays settled in Barnes County, hundreds of cars in the Northern Pacific yards in St. Paul were awaiting immigrants who were on their way to Dakota Territory. While many pioneers chose to travel by rail, others moved west by cov-ered wagon: "Many a pioneer came trudging along over the prairie with his oxen, his wagon laden with a tent, plow, a few handy tools, some simple furniture, the whole mounted with wife and children, while a cow or two, and perhaps some pigs brought up the rear."[3]

Had the Hallidays traveled by railroad, the Milwaukee and St. Paul would have carried them from Lake City — the nearest station to their farm — to St. Paul, and from there to Moorhead, Minnesota, and Valley City, Dakota Territory, by way of the Northern Pacific.[4] Both railroads were completed in the 1870s.[5] Following a common pioneer pattern, John Halliday may have made an exploratory journey alone before moving his family. Upon arrival, he would have visited the county courthouse, talked to local officials, and located the nearest land office. Then, with compass and plat map in hand, he would have walked or ridden on horseback to potential homestead sites. At the corners of each section, he would have found mounds of earth pierced with oak stakes marked with range, town-ship, and section numbers. If the land appeared to be fertile and promised a supply of water and fuel, he would have then filed his claim at the nearest land office.[6]

Land could be procured in a number of ways. Under the Preemption Act, land was purchased from the Northern Pacific Railroad or the federal government. In 1889, the year North Dakota became a state, railroad property, which lay in twenty-mile strips in alternate sections on either side of the track, cost three to six dollars an acre. If a settler borrowed cash to purchase railroad property, an interest rate of 7 percent, payable over a five- to ten-year period, would be tacked on.

Free land was also available under the terms of the Homestead Act. After paying an initial fourteen-dollar fee, 160 acres could be claimed free after five years if the settler cultivated a certain portion. Similarly, under the 1873 Timber Culture Act, 160 acres could also be claimed by planting ten acres in trees. At the end of an eight-year period, 675 trees had to be alive on each of ten acres in order to claim possession.[7]

The Hallidays arrived on the frontier seven years before North Dakota became a state. Only twelve years earlier, the white population had been estimated at not more than five hundred.[8] The Battle of Little Big Horn had taken place six years before, and the massacre at Wounded Knee lay eight years away. At the time of their arrival, the Hallidays would have found a pristine landscape, the grandeur of which must have captured their imaginations.

Barnes County, the Hallidays' destination, was first settled upon completion of a survey in 1872–73. The initial settlement was confined largely to the Sheyenne River Valley near Valley City. Most early settlers were of Irish, Scottish, or English background, and many of them were Canadians.[9]

Historian Thomas P. Elliott names two types of early settlers: those of limited funds who had to work for others before taking up land of their own, and bonanza farmers who operated thousands of acres requiring hundreds of men and women to run their farms.[10] Land deeds show that the Hallidays fell within a third category: people who, upon arrival, were able to settle on a homestead and begin farming at once.

Barnes County land deeds from the 1880s show that the Hallidays owned a 160-acre site in Alta township and a second section in Potter township. "Halliday Field," the name my sister and I gave to the Alta site, is a narrow strip of land bordered on the east by a prairie trail, a primitive road that once carried wagons and now accommodates farm machinery.

The rippling contour of Halliday Field reaches its highest point on the north; a small hill, piled with fieldstone and covered with shrubs, stands in the center.

Viewing the vista to the south, we sensed the awe that pioneers must have felt when they first saw the boundless Dakota prairie. Harry and Arlene Holm, who live on a farm adjacent to Halliday Field, told us it is doubtful that buildings were ever erected there. Had there been a house, it probably would have resembled the 1890, two-story, clapboarded frame structure with a central brick chimney that Mr. Holm was dismantling the day we made our visit.

Another awe-inspiring landscape is the Halliday site in section 24, Potter township, where the family homesteaded in 1886. An 1884 map shows that the area surrounding the Halliday farm was composed largely of small lakes and one former body of water named Dry Lake.[11] The Halliday homestead lay east of Dry Lake, north of the Hobart Trail, and overlooked an uncultivated hill. Because the Hallidays sought land that resembled English and Scottish landscapes, "Halliday Hill," as we named it, is another example of a vista that must have reminded the Hallidays of their earlier homes. In 1894, however, they sold their land to a Norwegian immigrant, Ole Olson, whose grandson Myron owns the farm today. When we interviewed Mr. Olson, he said that his home's central bay predates 1900, placing it within the Halliday era.[12]

The place the Hallidays called home was Sanborn, North Dakota, the town closest to the Potter site. Originally called "Sixth Siding," Sanborn was renamed in 1877 to honor the treasurer of the Northern Pacific. P. T. Barnum's brother I. W. Barnum was among the early settlers. Much of the surrounding land was owned by wealthy Minnesotans, including R. S. Munger, a Duluth elevator operator who owned twenty-six sections south of the town. Sanborn showed an early promise of becoming a booming trade center until the county seat was moved to Valley City in 1880. Further growth was hampered by major fires in 1885, 1923, and 1928.[13]

John and Anne Halliday's "Sanborn period" ended in 1894 when, for reasons unknown, they sold their farm. I have been unable to trace their whereabouts during the following five years. Beginning in 1899, they lived with their daughter and son-in-law, Mary and Warrington Brown, in Pipestone, Minnesota. John Halliday, the Scottish medical student, shoemaker, and farmer, died in Pipestone in 1906 at the age of ninety-one. In 1915,

The Halliday farmhouse in Sanborn, North Dakota, is a remodeled version of the Greek Revival upright temple form. According to its owner, Myron Olson, the kitchen and porch wings were added to the pre-1900 bay in the 1940s.

Anne Kilner Halliday, who had accompanied her husband on the sailing ship that brought the family to America in 1855, died at age ninety-one.

More is known about the North Dakota experiences of William, John Francis, and Marilla Holliday. William Holliday, John and Anne's oldest son, grew up on farms in Wisconsin and Minnesota. After he quit school in the third grade, William became a machinest and an inventor. As a result of seeing many farmers lose their limbs in farm machinery, William invented a self-feeding device for threshing machines. Several problems arose that doomed the potential success of this invention. One time while William was demonstrating his self-feeding model in a North Dakota wheat field, laborers, fearing the invention would jeopardize their jobs, sabotaged the machine by hiding rocks in the wheat bundles. Later, William patented several successful working models, but royalties promised him were lost in a tangle of legal disputes.[14]

John Francis Holliday, John and Anne's third child, was born in Wisconsin in 1859 and moved with his family to Lake City, Minnesota, in 1861. When he was a young man, he joined his brother William's McCormick-

Deering implement business near Devils Lake, North Dakota. To help his brother cover freight costs, John Francis organized an orchestra until an August freeze destroyed a bumper wheat crop, forcing William to close his business and return to Minnesota. John Francis, his wife, Jenny, and two daughters, Ruth and Francis, moved on to Sanborn to farm near John and Anne Halliday.[15]

In the summer of 1897, John Francis, his brother Ellsworth, and their families outfitted two covered wagons and left North Dakota to search for better land. The two families drove west into Montana, south into Wyoming, and then turned east into South Dakota. With the arrival of cold weather, they made their way back to North Dakota. Years later, John Francis's daughter Ruth wrote that the children had counted hundreds of buffalo skulls along the trail, a sign that native life in pioneer North Dakota had come to an end.[16]

That winter, John Francis's family lived in a deserted farmhouse near Sanborn. The following spring, they drove one hundred miles west to Kidder County, where John Francis found work as a threshing machine salesman. North of Tuttle, the family moved into a "bleak, unpainted, two story house" that, unfortunately, lay outside the boundaries of John Francis's legal claim. After moving the house, John Francis discovered that the legal land was dry. Until he could dig a well, water had to be hauled to the house on a stoneboat (a wooden sled used to haul rocks), an ordeal compounded by runaway horses, tipped barrels, and damage to the stoneboat. While John Francis was away, his wife and daughters milked cows, fed calves, sold butter, and cultivated flax.[17] A photograph of the Hollidays' farmhouse shows a white, clapboarded frame structure with plain window moldings and multipaned windows. A local farmer razed the house, a barn, and a coalhouse in 1954.[18] Although the original farmsite has disappeared, the prairie trail that runs east toward the distant hills remains today.

Early accounts of the history of northern Kidder County depict a rich social and cultural life coexisting with the daily struggle to survive. Social events often revolved around the Holliday Orchestra, which was in great demand for local dances.[19] John Francis was a cellist, his wife, Jenny, played the piano, and daughters Ruth and Francis were violinists. Besides being skilled as a musician, Ruth Holliday was also a photographer and a teacher. In 1913, Ruth and her husband, Walter, moved to Tuttle and

The prairie trail that once served as an entrance road to the farm is all that remains of the John F. Holliday homestead. A small depression to the right of the small tree shows where the farmhouse stood. Today, a small pond with scrubs and reeds provides wildlife shelter.

opened a restaurant, and in 1916, the couple built a town hall that included room for Ruth's photo studio and an auditorium to provide space for dances, roller skating, movies, and road shows.[20]

Stories of life in Kidder County during this time period were recorded by Viola Stramblad Liessman, whose brother, Theodore, married Francis Holliday. The story of the Stramblad family provides another rare glimpse into the lives of North Dakota pioneers at the turn of the century.[21]

In a reminiscence piece, Viola wrote that she, her mother, Carrie, and her brother, Theodore, sold their grocery store in Rockwell City, Iowa, and for three years traveled in Europe in search of a healthier climate for Theodore, who suffered from rheumatic fever. Around 1900, Viola heard about oil, gold, and lignite discoveries in North Dakota. When land syndicates and railroad representatives began providing cheap transportation to potential settlers, Viola purchased a twelve-dollar round-trip ticket and began what she later called the *"Greatest Adventure* possible for a girl — to own 160 acres of God's own virgin land." Upon arrival in North Dakota, Viola expected to see Indians and cowboys "a-horseback, wildly shooting into the air," but found instead a prosperous ranch where a former Iowa schoolteacher, now a "cowboy," offered to escort Viola to her claim (19–20).

After filing her claim in the summer of 1902, Viola returned to Iowa and moved her mother and brother to North Dakota. To support herself, Viola opened a millinery store in Jamestown but later leased it in order to return to "the wonderful wide open spaces." Theodore Stramblad initially had planned only a short visit but soon found his health so improved that he decided to stay permanently. After purchasing several buildings from a nearby ranch, Theodore borrowed sills to skid the buildings nine miles across the county's rough terrain. Using space in his home, Theodore opened a local post office, which he called "Bostonia" in honor of his alma mater, MIT. While his mother drove a team, Theodore dug holes and erected tamarack poles for the area's first telephone service, which he ran from a switchboard in his kitchen (20–21).

With a post office and later a store in place, Bostonia soon became a community center. Viola organized a literary club and, as a professional photographer, photographed bridal couples, Sunday school groups, homes, cattle, horses, and threshing crews. Bostonia also became the home of the Holliday Orchestra and the place where Francis Holliday met and in 1910 married Theodore Stramblad.

In her memoir, Viola described the positive aspects of life in Kidder County at that time: "Among these first homesteaders were university and college graduates, high class *musicians*, doctors, dentists, barbers, teachers and two blacksmiths, masons, carpenters — everything needed for a high class neighborhood" (31). She also noted the difficulties of living in a relatively primitive environment: "It took brave, courageous people to face this untried life . . . [and] no complaints about discomforts, weather, food, or bumps in the road [for] there were no roads" (31). Viola's memoir records prairie fires (one destroyed her mother's home), an encounter with an enraged bull, blinding blizzards, and a fifteen-year drought following World War I. When a promised railroad for Bostonia was built instead at Tuttle in 1911, Viola noted the beginning of a new and different era for northern Kidder County residents. Soon, many older people began commuting or moved into the growing towns. The arrival of the automobile, the need for more and better schools, as well as fires, deaths, and war forever changed the lives of rural North Dakota people (23). These and other conditions forced the Hollidays and Stramblads to eventually leave North Dakota.

The Stramblads and Hollidays chose Texas for their new home. In 1928, Theodore Stramblad built a trailer and began a sight-seeing and home-seeking journey that ended at Palacios on the Gulf Coast, where the family eventually settled on a ten-acre tract in the white-pine area north of Houston. Here, as if once again to begin the pioneer experience, the Stramblads built a log house. In the fall of 1938, John Francis and Jenny Holliday built a trailer and moved to Texas. The pioneer dream for John Francis, however, would not die. Twice he moved back to North Dakota, where he found the rigors of farming beyond his physical endurance. Returning to Texas, he died in 1944.

In 1907, William Holliday's daughter Marilla, who also dreamed of being a pioneer, returned to North Dakota, where she planned to establish a homestead claim. Years later, Marilla recorded her experience in a remarkable memoir that reveals the life of a single woman living in isolated pioneer conditions (appendix 4). Marilla Holliday was twenty-seven when she decided to leave Red Wing, Minnesota, to take up her claim. She wrote:

> Friends had given glowing accounts of living on a claim and my imagination painted an exciting and adventurous picture for me. I had, no doubt, inherited some of the pioneering spirit of my grandfather, who with his wife and infant daughter came to the middle east of Minnesota to teach and live among the Dakota Indians.[22]

Although Marilla's friends supported her quest, family members, with the exception of her father, discouraged her new endeavor: "my brother was convinced that I was the last person on earth to live alone, miles from civilization or another human being. His skepticism made me all the more determined to try or die. My father's willing acceptance of my plans was the only encouragement I received."

In April 1907, Marilla and her father set out for her 160-acre claim, which lay twenty-two miles from the Canadian border and sixteen miles from the village of Bowbells in Burke County, North Dakota. Marilla hired a young man from Bowbells, Wesley Johnson, to transport furniture and lumber for her claim shack. When Marilla and William followed Wesley by sleigh the next day, one of the horses broke through the ice on the snow-covered trail. Marilla became soaked while she led the horse to solid ground. Luckily, the pair reached a store four miles away where Marilla had a chance to dry out.

After spending a few days in a temporary shack, Wesley and William began building Marilla's house. Marilla's memoir shows her acute sense of the relation between shelter and landscape:

> My father and Wesley were getting ready to build my shack on top of a hill which sloped gently down to a lake shaped like an hourglass. While the men worked I took a look around. The land was flat, interrupted here and there by rolling hills. I had a far view from my little hill. Here and there and well distanced were some other shacks. Their snow-covered roofs blended into the white landscape; only walls swept clean by the wind and small windows protected by the roof gave them away as dwellings. Even in this vast desolate whiteness I could sense beauty and feel exhilaration because it was to be my land and my home.

Marilla's memoir also shows that Marilla was handy with a hammer and a saw. Wearing her father's fur coat over her own heavy coat, Marilla challenged Wesley to see who could shingle the fastest. Marilla wrote: "I looked like a bear rolling back and forth over the roof. . . . [Wesley] was a faster talker than worker, but we finished shingling the roof in good time as a 16 × 16 foot room did not present much of a problem."

Marilla provides a rare glimpse into a claim shanty interior:

> The inside walls were . . . covered with pink building paper. To complete the decor I sewed bedspreads, window curtains, hangings for a simulated closet, curtains for cupboards made from boxes, and a table cover. The yards and yards of cretonne of blue background with pink roses which I had purchased in Red Wing . . . made the room look very cheerful. There was suddenly an air of gaiety and summer inside. To complete the luxury I had one rocker, two straight chairs, and a table.

In order to make a comfortable bed, Marilla and William gathered bushels of cattails which they first shelled and then stuffed into mattress covers. A few days before his departure, William cleaned out a nearby spring and built the foundation, floor, and stud work for an add-on kitchen. After her father installed a laundry stove, Marilla lit the first fire as "a ceremonious event of great significance," for now she was warm for the first time in days. After completion of her living quarters, Marilla's neighbors approvingly dubbed her house "the palace." Marilla wrote that her father "wisely" left the kitchen for her to finish:

> Building the kitchen kept me busy from morning till night and I was grateful to my father for providing me with a project which left little time to feel lonesome. The kitchen was not exactly built according to Hoyle. The walls took on a gory appearance as I impartially sawed and pounded fingers as well as boards. I felt very proud of myself when the walls were up, the roof completed, and a sliding window put in, and then I discovered to my dismay that I had made no provision to enter the "palace" except by crawling through a window. This oversight was corrected by sawing through the wall from the living room, and no carpenter was ever so proud of his work as I was of that kitchen.

After her father's departure and with her house now completed, Marilla turned to her neighbors for company. In exchange for vegetables, milk, butter, and eggs, she agreed to tutor the children of her closest neighbors, the Wallaces, who lived two miles away. During storms, the children, Ruth and Donald, stayed overnight with Marilla. One day, while Marilla was working outdoors, a "heavily bearded man" appeared suddenly. The stranger, a Mr. Knapp, lived across the lake and "knew everyone in this part of North Dakota." During his first visit, Knapp sat on a rock outside Marilla's shanty telling stories about her neighbors, "every sentence spiced with profanity." Although put off by her first impression, Marilla said Knapp proved to be a kind neighbor.

In July, a girlhood friend, Adelaide Apfeld, arrived at Marilla's claim. During the night, a terrible windstorm swept across the prairie with such force that it ballooned the shanty walls. About midnight, a knock on the door announced a neighbor and her son who had crawled from their shanty after it had been lifted ten feet off its foundation. A month later, when a hailstorm riddled the tarpaper on Marilla's kitchen roof, she and Adelaide had to reshingle it the following day.

One fall day, Marilla and Ruth Wallace began the familiar five-mile walk to pick up the mail. Although fog was closing in, Marilla felt she knew the road so well she could walk it blindfolded. As the fog thickened, however, she discovered they were walking in circles, and she became panic-stricken: "Lost on the North Dakota prairie! I saw us forlorn and shivering, spending the cold night wandering, followed by packs of roaming coyotes whose weird laughterlike howling sent chills through my bones even when in the safety of my shack." Luckily, they heard footsteps and a neighbor's voice and were quickly led to safety.

Marilla originally had planned to return to Minnesota that October. However, when William arrived to take her home she learned that a new law forced settlers to reside continually on a claim for fourteen months or relinquish it. Although her father hoped she would return to Red Wing, Marilla decided she had to stay through the winter so as not to lose her claim. To prepare his daughter for the upcoming season, William gathered buckbrush and coal for heating, borrowed a horse and plow to dig a kitchen cellar, and cut fire furrows around the shanty and strip sod to pile against the shanty walls. The day before William left, the furrows saved Marilla's house from a prairie fire.

Marilla's memoir mentions encounters with local men, one fearful, the other a happy experience. One Sunday when she was invited to dinner, she met a man she calls "Matt from Bowbells," a boarder at the Wallaces'. Although she allowed Matt to drive her home in his "lovely sleigh and beautiful team of horses," she later told the Wallace children never to let Matt come to her place alone. However, a few days later, Matt slipped away from the children and made his way to Marilla's shanty.

> My welcome was not very cordial [Marilla wrote]; I let dinnertime pass by and it became quite evident that I had no intention to invite him for a meal. He finally left. He made a remark to the Wallaces about me to the effect that if I would only treat a man the way I treated my cat, I would be wonderful. . . . Matt did not stay for the winter; he packed up and went back to town.

Marilla's relationship with Wesley Johnson, though apparently brief, proved fun. One moonlit night, Johnson arrived at the shanty to ask Marilla to go coasting on scoop shovels. Accompanied by Ruth and Donald, who were staying the night, the four went up and down Marilla's hill. Marilla wrote:

> What fun this was! I doubt there has ever been so much laughter on this hill before or since. Happy hours like these made up for many lonely nights when howling coyotes seemed to be the only living things in

North Dakota. I would go to bed with my head covered to keep out the eerie high-pitched howling of these pitiful creatures that roamed the countryside in desperate search for food.

Marilla's homesteading experience nearly ended tragically, however. When her stovepipe fell as she was kindling the fire, Marilla tried to reach the place, thirteen feet above her head, where the pipe went through the roof. Although Marilla placed a chair atop her table, she still was unable to reach the hole. Finally, she threaded several lengths of pipe and carefully maneuvered them toward the hole: "I did not dare give up and tried it again and again. My hands were numb with cold, they didn't seem to belong to me, and my arms and shoulders were sore and tired. With one last desperate effort the pipe slipped through the hole."

At the end of fourteen months, Marilla "proved up" her claim by signing papers and celebrating with a dinner at the hotel in Bowbells with her father, who had arrived to help her pack her belongings for the trip back to Red Wing. Many of her neighbors gathered at the depot to say goodbye. Marilla wrote: "There was no time for sadness as the train pulled in and we departed. The laughing and shouting of good wishes by the many good friends I had found were long lingering in my ears as the train sped homeward."

Marilla Holliday spent most of the rest of her life living with her parents in Red Wing. To be near her relatives, she later moved to Texas, where, at age seventy, she married for the first time. Her husband, Bill Wauchope, was described to me as a "frontiersman-like cowboy."[23]

My Journey to Glencolumbkille, Ireland

To learn more about my Morgan heritage, I traveled to Ireland in the summer of 1988. As I was growing up, the only thing I knew about my paternal grandmother, Susan Maxwell, was that she was born in Glencolumbkille, County Donegal, in 1845, and that she had emigrated to America when she was twenty-two.[1] As I flew over the white-capped Irish Sea and first saw the green, orderly landscape below, I became acutely aware that I was my grandmother's sole descendant ever to return to Ireland.

To reach Glencolumbkille, I traveled one full day by bus from Dublin to Donegal, then by cab from Donegal to Malinmore, and finally by foot to Glencolumbkille, two miles away. When I walked into the village, the sky was a brilliant blue and filled with enormous billowy clouds. The road I traveled wound around the bay, which was dotted with island-sized rocks that jutted out into the ocean. I saw thistles and buttercups along the road, and the air was filled with the not-unpleasant odor of sheep manure. High above the road, sure-footed sheep grazed along the limestone outcrops.

The two-mile walk from Malinmore to Glencolumbkille provides us an extraordinary view of Donegal Bay.

During my bus trip from Dublin, I had seen no stone enclosure walls to speak of, but as I neared the village they suddenly appeared everywhere.

Upon arriving in Malinmore, I looked up the name "Maxwell" in the local directory, made several phone calls, and spoke briefly with the parish priest. Having had no luck with these contacts, I mentioned to the hotel clerk, Colette McDevitt, that I was researching family history. As it happened, Colette had worked as an intern at the Folk Village Museum, a reconstructed village representing three centuries of Glencolumbkille's history, where she had spent the previous summer compiling genealogies. She was sure that our family name had come up in her records. When I told her that I would be spending the day photographing local sites, she said she would try to get to the museum after leaving work and that she would search for documents related to the Maxwell family.

Meanwhile, my first stops in Glencolumbkille were the Catholic church on the village's main road and the Protestant Church of Ireland in the valley about a mile away. When I discovered that most of the Maxwell gravestones were in the Protestant graveyard, I made more phone calls and

Glencolumbkille is a quiet village of whitewashed stone buildings. The road from Malinmore passes the Catholic church (left) and a group of shops (right). Part of Glencolumbkille's prosperity stems from the sale of the world-famous Donegal wools. In the 1950s, Father James MacDyer formed a cooperative development project that created the excellent Folk Village Museum.

learned that in County Donegal Maxwell is a predominantly Protestant name. Sure enough, when I got back to Minnesota, my cousin Homer Martens said, "Of course you were on the right track — your grandmother was a Protestant. In fact, she left Ireland to seek religious freedom."

After an exhilarating day, I returned to the hotel, satisfied that I had seen the village and that perhaps I had discovered my grandmother's parish church. At the hotel desk, I found that Colette had left a message saying that she had information that she knew I would want to see. When she arrived, Colette showed me a copy of my grandmother's birth cer-

The Protestant Church of Ireland stands somewhat removed from the heart of the village. An ecclesiastical structure was built on this site as early as the 800s. In 1842, a souterrain (underground passage) was discovered. Believed to have been a hideout for clergy in the days of Viking raids, the passage runs under the Protestant graveyard. The present edifice was constructed in 1827.

tificate with her parents' names — William Maxwell and Eleanor Crawford — and her place of birth — Faugher, County Donegal.

Where was Faugher? Was I in the wrong village? No, Colette assured me, Faugher was a "townland," a subdivision of the village proper. In fact, I had walked through Faugher while searching for gravestones at the Church of Ireland. Although I was now armed with new information, dusk was rapidly approaching. Glencolumbkille and Faugher lay two miles away. Knowing that my time was extremely limited, I begged a ride from the first person I saw in front of the hotel — a man in a pickup truck. Although the driver was worried that he might be late for evening Mass, he dropped me off ten minutes later at the crossroads leading to Faugher.

As I walked up the hill, once again passing the Protestant church, I stopped people returning home from an earlier Mass to ask where I could find Faugher. I was told that I was in Faugher, an area of open fields and one modern dwelling. When I asked the owner of the lone house if there were other structures thereabouts, he pointed toward a cluster of buildings down a narrow path. The open fields, the owner's house, and the structures down the path, he told me, formed the townland of Faugher.

I could not believe my eyes when I saw a white-plastered thatched cottage where the path ended. Earlier in the day, at the Folk Museum, I had walked through a house that represented a dwelling common to the area in 1850, but here was the real thing. I knocked at the door, hoping someone was home. When the door opened, an elderly man of medium height wearing a hat and worn-thin work clothes peered out at me. Although he seemed suspicious, the man listened while I told him why I was there. He said his name was Joe McGinley and asked me if I was a relative. He told me that an American named McGinley had visited him a number of years before searching for his Irish ancestors. By now I was standing in the parlor while Mr. McGinley searched in the back room for a letter he had saved from the American visitor.

Sitting in front of a peat fire in the parlor was another man whom Joe introduced as his older brother George. Although I was in the house no longer than fifteen minutes, I'll never forget either the room or the man sitting by the fire. George had a round red face, a full mouth, large round eyes, and bristly gray whiskers. His stocky build suggested that he had once been extremely strong. Although the room was very hot, George wore a wool cap, dark work clothes, and heavy work boots. When I tried to strike up a conversation with George while Joe continued searching for the letter, he only stared straight ahead wordlessly.

Silently, I tried to memorize everything in the room. Like the exterior, the interior features resembled the 1850 dwelling at the Folk Museum. In striking similarity to the model cottage, the McGinleys' parlor was small, low-ceilinged, and oriented toward the tiny fireplace with its gray tile surround and a well cut low into the wall. The fire gave out intense heat. This, I thought, was a room to huddle down in on a cold winter's day. Against the wall to the left of the fireplace was a dresser, on whose upper shelves dishes were set on end, facing forward, angled downward, and braced by wooden rungs. A narrow window next to the door let in the only source of light. Seemingly, this room had not changed in over 130 years — and people were still living in it! Was it possible that this cottage was Grandmother Maxwell's home and this the very room she last saw before leaving for America?

By the time I left the house, darkness was rapidly approaching. Light

The McGinley cottage resembles the 1850 structure at the Folk Village Museum that Aidan Manning calls an example of the "best" house of its time. The village cottage has two rooms and a loft, plastered and whitewashed stone walls, bog-oak rafters, and a flagstone floor. Many of these same features appear in the McGinley cottage.

and time had run out before I could study the exterior and examine the outbuildings, including a thatched-roof shed built of stone. When I had first approached the house, I had interrupted Joe in the process of freshly thatching the stone shed; as I left, he was walking back to the shed to continue his work.

I left Faugher in a daze. With but faint light in the sky, I had ahead of me a long walk back to the hotel. Pausing once more at the church, I saw figures standing in the graveyard — three young girls and a man about my age talking to an elderly man. The older man had parked his bicycle by the church wall. Two pails of fresh milk hung, yoke-style, on either side of his bike. The men appeared to be old friends who had not seen each other for some time. While the men were engaged in deep conversation, the girls romped in the graveyard. When I saw that the younger man had an automobile, I asked politely if I could hitch a ride back to the hotel. As if to let me know that he didn't want to be rushed, he said, "If you continue walking, I'll catch up with you." I had walked about a mile when the man, his wife (whom I had not seen previously), and their three daughters pulled up beside me. As I got in the car, the couple introduced themselves as Sydney and Dorothy Blain from Dublin and said they lived during the summer in Sydney's ancestral home in Malinmore. Later in the evening, all of us got together in the hotel pub for drinks.

I left Glencolumbkille satisfied merely to have walked where my ancestors had walked before me. The fortuitous meetings with Colette McDevitt, the McGinleys, and the Blains gave me an opportunity to briefly experience my ancestors' culture firsthand. Standing in the McGinley cottage equaled the thrill of my first visit to my maternal grandmother's home, Field Head. I left Glencolumbkille with a deep respect for my father's ancestors and their native land. A passage from the writings of Sir Arnold Bax mirrors the feelings I had the day I left County Donegal:

> I like to fancy that on my deathbed my last vision in this life will be the scene from my window on the upper floor at Glencolumbkille, of the still, brooding, dove-grey mystery of the Atlantic at twilight; the last glow of sunset behind Glen Head . . . the calm slope of Scraig Beefan, its glittering many-coloured surface of rock, bracken and heather, now one uniform purple glow.[2]

Most historical accounts of Glencolumbkille cite the beauty of the landscape, the religious and archaeological significance of the area, and the difficulties people have had making a living. Situated in a valley, the village is blocked from the ocean by hills to the west, but north-south roads provide villagers with a magnificent view of the rock-dotted western coast.

Glencolumbkille escaped most of the turmoil created by the Plantation of Ulster (1610), the importation of Scottish and English settlers who created Ireland's tenant system. By 1659, only three people of Scottish and English descent had settled in the village. The rent rolls of 1784 list the earliest Maxwells in Glencolumbkille, and a William and a James Maxwell were recorded in the nearby townland of Straide.[3]

The population of Glencolumbkille tripled between 1774 and 1830. When the area's natural resources could no longer sustain this growth, landlords took advantage of this condition and began "to squeeze every earthly possession from their tenantry and then evict."[4] The years between the Great Famine and the 1880s were particularly harsh in Donegal. Manning quotes Thomas C. Foster's *Letters on the Condition of the People of Ireland*, describing the cottages of John and Charles M'Cabe in 1846:

> They were stone-built, and well roofed — but the mud floor was uneven, damp and filthy. In one corner was a place for the pig, with a drain from it through the wall to carry [off] the liquid manure, like a stable. Two chairs, a bedstead of the rudest description, a cradle, a spinning-wheel and an iron pot constituted the whole furniture. An inner room contained another rude bedstead; the mud floor was quite damp. In this room six children slept on loose hay, with one dirty blanket to cover them. The father, mother, and an infant slept in the first room, also on loose hay, and with but one blanket on the bed. The children were running about as nearly naked as possible, dressed in the cast-off rags of the mother and father; the father could not buy them clothes. They have not been to mass for a twelvemonth for the want of decent clothes to go in. . . . I give you these as examples, without any kind of selection, of the universal condition of the tenantry.[5]

Accounts of conditions in mid-nineteenth-century Donegal underscore the miracle of Susan Maxwell's survival. Susan was born in the midst of the potato famine, and during the first four years of her life, Irish society suffered famine as well as successive epidemics of typhus, cholera, relapsing fever, and scurvy. Damp conditions in cottages, as described above, caused a disease called small fever, and where lice were common, cottage dwellers developed typhus and relapsing fever. Manning estimates that the population of Glencolumbkille in 1851 should have exceeded 5,000 but reached only 3,881.[6] These statistics suggest major reasons why so many Irish left their homeland. Although I may never know all the reasons why Grandmother Maxwell left Ireland, personal, social, economic, and religious motives undoubtedly combined to hasten her departure.

12

My Father's Story

After my journey to Ireland, I turned my attention to the Morgan side of the family.[1] Because my father had died before I was born, and since I had had only limited contact with his family, the search for my father's heritage assumed a special meaning. According to family stories, I knew that my father's mother, Susan Maxwell, had arrived in America in 1867 and that after a brief stay in Illinois had moved to Story County, Iowa, where she met Joseph Homer Morgan. Joseph's first wife, Mary Seaton, had recently died of tuberculosis, leaving behind her husband and a year-old son, Homer Lorenzo Morgan. After a brief courtship, Susan and Joseph married, and in 1870 the couple took up farming on an eighty-acre site in Sherman township near Colo, Iowa.[2]

I began the search for my Morgan heritage by driving to Iowa to search for Joseph and Susan Maxwell Morgan's farm. Driving five miles north of Colo on arrow-straight Highway 65, I made a ninety-degree right turn and, within a mile, found a modern ranch-style farmhouse and a well-maintained cluster of metal outbuildings. So modern was my grand-

Joseph Homer Morgan (1841–1912) was a successful farmer who raised Percheron horses on his farm in Pipestone County.

Susan Maxwell Morgan (1845–1917) emigrated to Cherry Valley, Illinois, from County Donegal, Ireland, when she was twenty-two. After her marriage to Joseph Homer Morgan in 1870, she gave birth to seven children, all of whom survived her.

parents' place that I found not even one foundation stone from the 1870s farm. As I drove around Sherman township, I discovered other local farms that resembled the uncluttered yard and well-kept buildings on my grandparents' site.

In 1882, Joseph and Susan left Iowa and moved to the treeless prairie of Sweet township, Pipestone County, and in 1887 to nearby Eden township, a mile from the tiny village of Ihlen.[3] After purchasing three hundred additional acres, Joseph named his second place Excelsior Stock Farm and began raising Percherons and large grain crops that required steam engines, water wagons, and sleeping shacks for harvest hands.[4]

My father, Will Morgan, was born on the Sweet township farm in 1883. He attended rural schools and, like most farm children at that time, attended class only sporadically because he was needed at home. In 1898, however, the family moved into Pipestone, where in 1904 Will graduated

This ca. 1883 photograph shows a cross-gabled, T-shaped farmhouse owned by Joseph and Susan Morgan. The central figures are Susan (holding William Towner) and her husband, Joseph. The men on either side are hired hands. According to grandson Homer Martens, when the house was new the family slept upstairs and kept horses and cows downstairs. The remodeled farmhouse and a chicken coop are the only remaining structures from the Morgan period.

from high school. The summer after graduation, he managed a department store and later clerked in banks in Trosky, Minnesota, and Doon, Iowa. Completing his banking apprenticeship, he entered the First National Bank of Pipestone, where, during the following twenty-seven years, he advanced from cashier to vice president, the office he held at the time of his death in 1933. According to family stories, my father was driven to succeed. In the words of his son-in-law Bill Forman, "[Will] was always busy; the bank was his life."[5]

Will's son Alan believes his father had an excellent rural and high school education and that he was endowed with superior intelligence:

> [Dad's] ability to work in mathematics was sheer wizardry. Whether this was innate or acquired I do not pretend to know, but since the banker had only two tools in that day, the simple adding machine and the typewriter, then a principal requisite for banking was the ability to compute — and often very quickly and mentally. Dad had that trait outstandingly.[6]

At the turn of the century, Pipestone High School offered a curriculum that included Latin, German, English, history, the sciences, mathematics, algebra, geometry, and physics.[7] Will took two years of Latin and two years of German. The option to study German was a distinct advantage to a person about to enter business in ethnic southwestern Minnesota. According to Alan,

> Dad was surely proficient in German. Although his family picked up a little German . . . since so many German settlers had come in a few years after the English originally settled the land. But Dad added to that environmental start a real groundwork in German gained in high school. I am absolutely certain that he spoke more correct German than he did English. . . . I have heard him many times speak to German buyers at farm sales . . . with perfect fluency and understanding.[8]

Will's proficiency in language was matched by his abilities on the football field and the wrestling mat. My brothers have often told me about our father's competitive spirit, a trait appreciated during an era when the reputation of a small-town sports figure often reached legendary heights. V-wedge football, in particular, was a sport Will played with ferocity.[9] Will also wrestled in the tradition of Farmer Burns and Frank Gotch, contemporary heroes of that ancient sport. Even after age forty, Will wrestled with the Prunty brothers, one of whom was an Olympic star.[10] In Alan's words,

> Dad loved competition, and I think that he sublimated and compensated and ripped away frustrations . . . when he wrestled with these

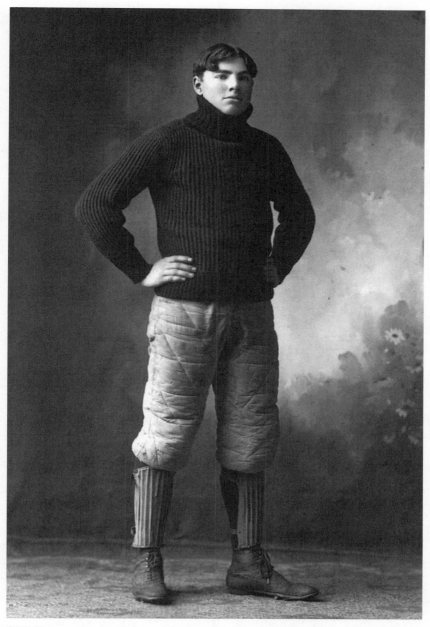

Will Morgan, who played left guard for the undefeated 1902 and 1903 Pipestone High School football teams, was a fierce competitor in several sports.

good friends. . . . And so he could wrestle. I know that personally. I have worked with him, and he tied me into every kind of knot that sailors used to have to master. He worked me over but really good. He creamed me. He just politely wrestled me down and out, and was all over me like a thundershower or more like a load of hay that breaks its towline, drops on your head, and neatly breaks your neck in turn. He could wrestle.[11]

After Stan left for college, Will transformed Stan's bedroom into a gymnasium by emptying the room of furniture, covering the floor with sawdust, and nailing a canvas cover to the oak flooring, the holes of which are visible today.[12]

Although I never knew my father, I learned to love and admire him through the stories told to me by my sister and brothers. A favorite family story concerns our parents' courtship. During their high school years, Will occasionally dated Mabelle Brown, who was three years younger than her future husband. Once, during her senior year, Mabelle and a male friend went to a dance in the nearby village of Woodstock. When this news reached Will, he hitched up a team, drove to Woodstock, and willfully brought home the woman who, in 1910, would become his wife.

After my mother graduated from high school, she and her sister Anne spent one year at the University of Minnesota's College of Agriculture. That year was a turning point for the sisters, who talked about their university experiences for the rest of their lives. According to Anne and Mabelle, their father insisted that his daughters would have to return home at the end of the year because he believed the city was too dangerous for young women.[13]

Mother never forgot the university or the rich cultural life she discovered in St. Paul. She always remembered attending a downtown play where she saw Maude Adams and for years reminisced about her own role in a campus production of *The Mikado*. Mother always dreamed of returning to the university to pursue a career in architecture or interior design. Denied this opportunity, Mother never fully accepted her role as a homemaker.

My parents were married in my grandparents' home in the summer of 1910. As I was growing up, my siblings told me stories about the happy times my parents experienced during their early years of marriage. Will

This photograph of the Paynesville depot near Lake Koronis, Minnesota, is a family icon. After their wedding ceremony on August 3, 1910, Will and Mabelle Morgan took the midnight train from Pipestone, arriving at dawn in Paynesville. The newlyweds spent the following month honeymooning at Lake Koronis.

and Mabelle spent their honeymoon at a resort on Lake Koronis, Minnesota, an event recorded in a photograph album that sat on our coffee table when I was a child. The little wooden depot in Paynesville, Minnesota, where the dusty travelers stepped off the train from Pipestone, is a familiar icon from this album.

Will and his only daughter, my sister, Courtenay, had a very special relationship. Even today, at age eighty-three, Courtenay tells me that she still misses her father. When she was a child, Courtenay caught her foot in a metal pail. When Will was unable to free it, he said, "I guess we'll have to cut it off." Courtenay recalls how terrified she was thinking Will meant her foot! Another time, Will saved Courtenay's life when she was choking on mashed potatoes. Holding Courtenay upside down by her feet, Will slapped her hard on the back until the obstruction shot across the room.[14] Courtenay remembers that when she was older her father took her on insurance-selling trips around the county. As they drove home after dark, Will would recite poems, including his favorite: William Cullen Bryant's "Thanatopsis." In her memoir, Courtenay described her father as "tall, [with] auburn hair, always dieting... A beautiful person, honest to a fault. I never heard him say anything or tell anything off-color."[15] Courtenay has told me other treasured fragments about her relationship with our father. Courtenay remembers Will inviting her as a teenager to eat lunch with him in the elegant dining room of the Calumet Hotel, where Will would occasionally arrange to have a young man accompany them. In 1930, Will borrowed from his life insurance policy to send Courtenay to a fashionable school, Stephens College, in Columbia, Missouri. Before she left home, the cedar chest she had received as a high school graduation gift was crated and loaded on the train that carried Courtenay to Missouri. My sister remembers asking her roommate to read her father's letters because they were written in an illegible, though beautiful, script. When Will and Alan made a special trip to visit Courtenay in Missouri, Will bought her a three-piece suit, hat, gloves, shoes, and silk stockings.[16]

My brothers Alan and Stan also have fond memories of our father. Alan remembers that when bank customers gave Will boxes of cigars as Christmas gifts he would smoke them until they were gone, usually by April, and then not touch another one until the following December.[17]

Stan recalls that our father also chewed tobacco, but only during fishing trips.[18] Will also loved expensive and fashionable clothes. Alan remembers accompanying his father to Minneapolis, where, in a day when an ordinary suit cost $30, Will would order a tailor-made one costing $125.[19]

Many of the family stories that I grew up hearing revolve around early automobiles and fishing trips. During the 1920s, the family made annual fishing trips to either Lake Koronis or Leech Lake. According to my brother Stan, "In the earliest of Dad's time he used a Ford Model T touring car (it had a cloth top that let down) which belonged to the bank. The family sat in this car on the night that World War I ended. It was parked in front of the Calumet [Hotel], where Kaiser Wilhelm was hanged in effigy from the sign which was attached to the building."[20]

Courtenay and my brother Loran remember one family car equipped with a rear rack that held a large steamer trunk filled with what our mother considered "essential" camping supplies. Mother took along everything, they said, except a can opener and a paring knife. The trip home over Minnesota's unimproved roads was often an unpleasant experience, however, especially when the children's sunburned backs rubbed up against the horsehair seats of the family's Willys-Knight.[21]

Our family has an almost mystical connection with Leech Lake, a northern Minnesota lake in the Chippewa National Forest. For five generations, the Morgan family has traveled to Leech to rest, read, sightsee, and fish for walleyes and northerns. Besides these activities, Leech Lake's pristine beauty forms part of our family's folklore. On any one day the sunlit shoreline may be drenched in a palette of orange, red, and yellow, but on the next day, the lake may be shrouded in a mist where, miragelike, distant boats seem suspended above the water.

Stan and Will sometimes traveled alone to Leech Lake. In the days before the widespread use of outboard motors, Will would row while Stan trolled for walleyes. At other times they hired an Indian guide to row them five miles to the walleye holes around Bear Island. One year, to his horror, Stan accidentally dropped into the lake a ten-dollar gold piece our dad had given him.

As banks began folding all across the United States in the late 1920s and early 1930s, Will's concern for the First National Bank's stability intensified. Stan and Courtenay remember that officers from the rival Security

Bank asked Will's bank to lend them money to help buttress their failing institution. Courtenay said, "Dad suffered over the closing of the Security Bank but could not see his way to buy them out, although the officers begged him, pleaded, to keep it open."[22] After attending Macalester College in St. Paul for two years, Stan was forced to leave school and come home to work in the bank because Will could no longer afford to pay his tuition. As a young teller, Stan remembers that because his father feared a run on the bank, he sent an officer to Sioux Falls to exchange $10,000 in large currency for ten thousand one-dollar bills. When customers queued up the following day to withdraw their savings, the cashiers slowly issued the smaller bills until customers tired of standing in line. In the days to follow, customers began returning to the bank to redeposit their one-dollar bills.[23]

By December 1932, the underlying stress caused by the Depression had caught up with Will. There are many versions of the events that led up to his death in January 1933. Sometime late in December, Loran and Will went pheasant hunting on a local farm. Loran recalled that "[Dad] got scratched on a barbed wire fence. Later, he treated it with after-shave lotion. From the scratch, he developed an infection, and from that meningitis."[24]

The story of my father's death, as told to me by my mother, is as follows. On top of the infected barbed-wire cut, Will caught a severe case of influenza around Chrismas and for several days was confined to bed. Although he had not fully recovered, Will felt compelled to return to work. After working New Year's Day, he came home completely exhausted, relapsed from the flu, and contracted meningitis. For two weeks, he slipped in and out of a coma until his death on January 14.

At my father's funeral, the local minister summarized his life in this way:

> Mr. Morgan was perhaps the most popular man in Pipestone, but he did not seek popularity. He enjoyed none of the tricks of the professional good fellow. He was not a man about town. He was not a hale fellow well met. He was not the glad hand, back slapping type of man. His popularity did not spring from the surface. It was rooted in deeper soil. . . . It was the popularity based upon real worth, difficult to explain because the profoundest realities of life are usually the simplest.[25]

I treasure the family stories that touch upon my father's life. In the eyes of my brothers and my sister, my father is a heroic figure. Not having known him, I share this feeling, perhaps even to a greater degree. Mother never accepted my father's death, I feel, for rarely did she speak of him. Her grief was never resolved, perhaps, so closely twined were my birth and his death.

CONCLUSION AND FAMILY ALBUM

I wrote this book not only to understand and appreciate the lives of my ancestors but also to understand myself. I hope this book will reach future generations and help them to understand our family's heritage.

I used my ancestors' material culture to bring the past back to life. The salt lantern, which I first saw at a very early age, helped form my interest in my family's history. The death of my father before I was born and my raising by a single parent have made my personal heritage unique and challenging.

At some point in my career, I listened to my inner voice and began the task of collecting, interpreting, and writing the history that has shaped my own life. I took seemingly small and insignificant objects from my ancestral past and searched for the stories that would expand upon and explain them. To achieve my objective, I tried to place myself within my ancestors' surroundings. Life, of course, was very different for my ancestors from the way it has been for me. Through their material culture, however, I have begun to see their lives more vividly. I believe I have captured some of my own feelings and, perhaps, captured some of the unexpressed feelings of those who came before me.

Anne Kilner Halliday (1824–1915) was born at Field Head, a farm in Westmorland County, England. Although her father disapproved of her courtship with a "lowly Scotsman," Anne married John Halliday and emigrated to America in 1855.

In this photograph, John Halliday (1815–1906) appears stern and aloof, characteristics fostered by his Scottish Calvinistic upbringing. In the journal he kept during his voyage to America, John Halliday reveals other traits — courage, a sense of humor, and intellectual curiosity.

Mary Halliday Brown (1847–1938) was born at Field Head and came to America with her parents and her brother, William. During the six-week ocean journey, Mary and William survived illnesses that took the lives of several other children. Mary met her future husband, Warrington Brown, in Goodhue County, Minnesota. Her granddaughter, Courtenay Morgan-Forman, recalls that Grandmother Brown "probably did not weigh ninety-eight pounds, wringing wet."

After he left farming in 1898, Grandfather Brown started a John Deere implement business in Pipestone. His grandson Stan Morgan remembers the buggy whips (center, left) that hung in the shop years after John Deere developed gasoline tractors (photograph ca. 1915).

Because she was too shy to recite, Anne Belle Brown Winters (1883–1971) quit school in the tenth grade but later took courses in home economics at the University of Minnesota. In Pipestone, Anne taught piano and violin, wrote fiction, and read literature and history but returned to the university in her midthirties to study music and creative writing. A genteel, well-bred woman, Anne surprised her family when she married George Woodruff Winters, a cowhand, railroad worker, and farmer.

Mabelle Brown (1887–1964) attended the University of Minnesota in 1905 and aspired to become an architect or an interior designer. Because her father believed cities were evil, Mabelle was forced to return home at the end of her freshman year. In 1910, she married her high school sweetheart, raised five children, and lived in Pipestone the remainder of her life.

This photograph shows the children of four of the Brown siblings: Courtenay Morgan, Janet Brown (Garfield's daughter), Paul Donaldson, Stan Morgan behind Rod Brown (Paul's son), Loran Morgan, Alan Morgan, and Philip Brown (Garfield's son).

In this snapshot, I am standing in the yard between Grandfather's and my house holding Grandfather's pith helmet. Grandfather and I often sat on his porch, where he promised to take me to northern Minnesota in his horse and wagon.

This photograph was taken during the early years of World War II. The place is the front lawn of my grandparents' house, which by 1938 belonged to Uncle George and Aunt Anne Winters. On the cracked sidewalk we children jump-roped, roller-skated, rode bikes, and hop-scotched. Three generations are shown here: George and Anne Winters, Alan, Mabelle, and Bill Morgan (back row); unknown child, Anne Kilner Winters, unknown child, and Victoria Rose Winters (front row).

The Morgan house was influenced by mail-order architecture, the Craftsman tradition, and the Prairie style. Its strongest architectural features are its use of bracketed overhangs and an abundance of windows. Greater architectural merit would have been achieved had the builder designed the windows in bands and used fieldstone for the foundation and chimney stack.

Brig. Gen. George J. Stannard fought in major engagements of the Civil War from Bull Run to Petersburg. Once captured and five times wounded, this citizen-soldier proved to be one of the Union's ablest officers. Courtesy of the Vermont Historical Society, Montpelier.

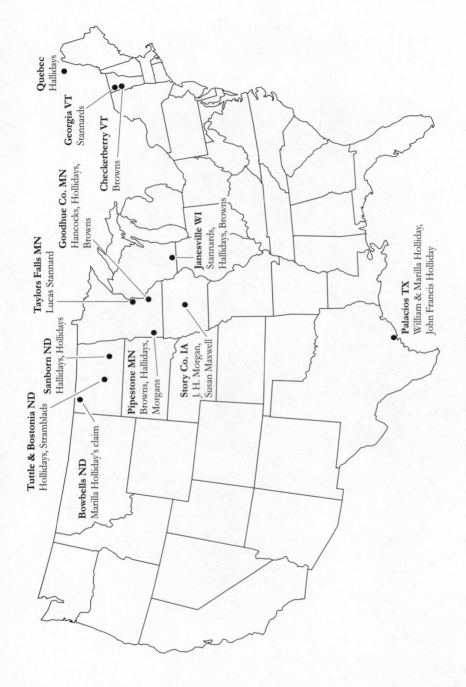

Quebec
Hallidays

Georgia VT
Stannards

Checkerberry VT
Browns

Goodhue Co. MN
Hancocks, Hollidays,
Browns

Janesville WI
Stannards,
Hallidays, Browns

Taylors Falls MN
Lucas Stannard

Sanborn ND
Hallidays, Hollidays

Pipestone MN
Browns, Hallidays,
Morgans

Story Co. IA
J. H. Morgan,
Susan Maxwell

Palacios TX
William & Marilla Holliday,
John Francis Holliday

Turtle & Bostonia ND
Hollidays, Stramblads

Bowbells ND
Marilla Holliday's claim

FAMILIES IN AMERICA.

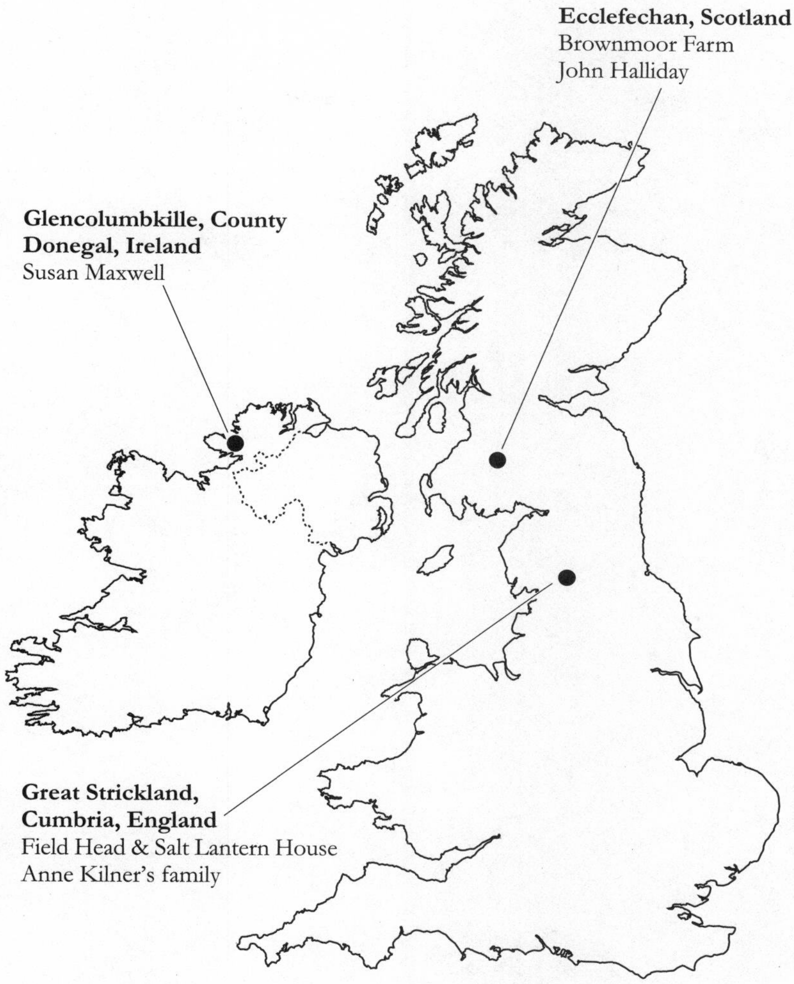

Ecclefechan, Scotland
Brownmoor Farm
John Halliday

**Glencolumbkille, County
Donegal, Ireland**
Susan Maxwell

**Great Strickland,
Cumbria, England**
Field Head & Salt Lantern House
Anne Kilner's family

FAMILIES IN THE BRITISH ISLES.

FAMILY HOUSES AND FARMS

House or Farm	Place	Date of Construction	Style	Landscape Description	1990s Condition
Brownmoor	Ecclefechan, Scotland	1750?–1830	Georgian	Hilly terrain	House occupied; service bldgs.; fair
Field Head	Great Strickland, Cumbria Co., England	1750?–1796	Longhouse tradition	Pennine Chain	Active farm; excellent
Salt Lantern House	Great Strickland	1840	Gothic Revival	Village lot	Excellent
Maxwell-McGinley Farm	Glencolumbkille, Ireland	1850s	Thatched cottage	Rocky seacoast	Active farm; excellent
Samuel Stannard House	Franklin Co., VT	1794	Log	Flat farmland	Razed
Amos Brown Farmhouse	Colchester, VT	1820–1840	Greek Revival	Spring, gorge, orchard	Good
Gen. Geo. J. Stannard House	Milton, VT	1823	Greek Revival	Flat farmland	In path of industrial development
Stannard-Stark Farm	Janesville, WI	1853–1883	Greek Revival	Flat farmland	Excellent
John & Anne Halliday Farm	Goodhue Co., MN	1860s–1916	Vernacular L	Mississippi bluff	Razed, 1916
Wm. & Marilla Holliday Farm	Goodhue Co., MN	1860–1920	Queen Anne T	Mississippi bluff	Destroyed, 1980s

	Location	Date	Style	Setting	Condition
W. B. Brown Farm	Goodhue Co., MN	1860s	Unknown (frame?)	Hillcrest, rolling farmland	Razed
Sweet Claim Shanty & Soddy	Pipestone Co., MN	1878	Wood/earth	Town lot	Razed; museum replication (shanty)
Brown-Blom Farm	Pipestone Co., MN	1879	Greek Revival T	Rolling prairie	Poor
Jos. Homer Morgan Farmhouse	Pipestone Co., MN	c1887	Cross-gabled T	Prairie	Good; remodeled
W. B. & Mary Brown House	Pipestone	1898	Prairie Cube–Eastlake	Town lot	Fair (moved)
W. T. & Mabelle Morgan House	Pipestone	1918–1919	Craftsman	Town lot	Restored
Anne Winters's Music Studio	Pipestone	1932	Cottage	Town lot	Good
Halliday-Olson Farm	Sanborn, ND	c1880s	Greek Revival	Overlooks Halliday Hill	Fair to good; remodeled
John F. Holliday Farm	Kidder Co., ND	1897–1954	Unknown	Rolling hills	Razed
Marilla Holliday Claim Shanty	Burke Co., ND	1907	Frame shanty	Unknown	Razed
Lucas Stannard–Grossmann House	Taylors Falls, MN	1854–1891	Greek Revival–Victorian	Waterfall & ravine	Restored

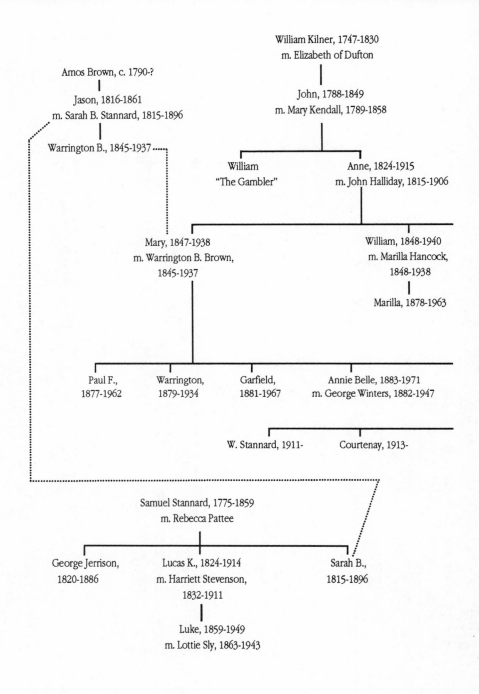

William Kilner, 1747-1830
m. Elizabeth of Dufton

Amos Brown, c. 1790-?

Jason, 1816-1861
m. Sarah B. Stannard, 1815-1896

John, 1788-1849
m. Mary Kendall, 1789-1858

Warrington B., 1845-1937

William
"The Gambler"

Anne, 1824-1915
m. John Halliday, 1815-1906

Mary, 1847-1938
m. Warrington B. Brown,
1845-1937

William, 1848-1940
m. Marilla Hancock,
1848-1938

Marilla, 1878-1963

Paul F.,
1877-1962

Warrington,
1879-1934

Garfield,
1881-1967

Annie Belle, 1883-1971
m. George Winters, 1882-1947

W. Stannard, 1911-

Courtenay, 1913-

Samuel Stannard, 1775-1859
m. Rebecca Pattee

George Jerrison,
1820-1886

Lucas K., 1824-1914
m. Harriett Stevenson,
1832-1911

Sarah B.,
1815-1896

Luke, 1859-1949
m. Lottie Sly, 1863-1943

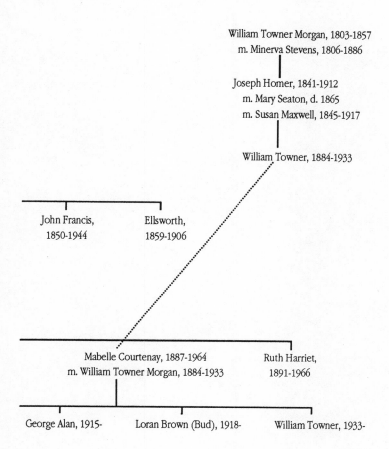

William Towner Morgan, 1803-1857
m. Minerva Stevens, 1806-1886

Joseph Homer, 1841-1912
m. Mary Seaton, d. 1865
m. Susan Maxwell, 1845-1917

William Towner, 1884-1933

John Francis,   Ellsworth,
1850-1944   1859-1906

Mabelle Courtenay, 1887-1964   Ruth Harriet,
m. William Towner Morgan, 1884-1933   1891-1966

George Alan, 1915-   Loran Brown (Bud), 1918-   William Towner, 1933-

APPENDIX I. "Weighed in the Balance"

This unpublished manuscript was written by Annie (Anne) Belle Winters, summer 1944.

My dear nephew William T.,

And I mean "nephew," not once or twice removed.

I am writing to you this morning because you are a "lie-a-bed" as my grandmother, Anne Kilner Halliday, used to say.

I believe you would be interested to know such things as I know (or have been told) about your kin on the maternal side of the house.

It is hard for me to find time to write because I am very busy with my grandchildren, Anne Kilner Winters, 4½ years old and her one-year-old sister, Victoria Rose Winters. They are your cousins, second or once-removed for ought I know.

Anne Kilner Halliday was the great-great grandmother of this small Anne Kilner Winters, named for Anne Kilner Halliday.

I think to start right I should go even further back than *your* great-grandparents, William and Mary Kilner and the parents of Anne Kilner Halliday's husband, who was John Halliday.

I'd like to tell you right now about the courtship of Anne Kilner and John Halliday, but you know "first things first."

So we'll start with John Halliday's parents. I do not know their first names but their last name was *not* Holliday. It was Halliday — HALLIDAY. When your great-grandfather John Halliday came to the U.S.A., the people here thought he called himself "Holliday." So they called him that and after a while he wrote it that way. . . .

These Hallidays lived very near a peat-bed so when they wanted fuel they had it free. They cut [it] in blocks and piled it up to dry. When dry enough, it was ready to burn. It was a good thing they had it, as they were quite lacking in money. (Perhaps they were very wealthy in mind and spirit as so many Scotch people are. Anyway they were strongly religious and, of course, strictly honest.)

Gt. gramp J. H. very much desired an education. So an uncle of his decided to help J. H. to become a doctor. After J. H. had studied a short time, the uncle died and J. H. had to learn to be a shoe-maker. Now that seems just too bad, but don't forget the warp and the woof. It was no doubt (I think anyhow) planned that J. H. should be the village shoe-maker so that he should meet Anne Kilner. Otherwise we, as we are, wouldn't be here! What do *you* think?

Well then, our ancestors, the Hallidays, were Scotch people. They lived in the "Low-lands" not far north of the English border. They lived at Eccelfachen. (I've forgotten how to spell that but no doubt your mother can correct it here_____.) It is pronounced EKKEL-FAHEN (almost, anyway, but with a Scotch accent). That is the city where the great author, Thomas Carlyle, was born. Your great-grandfather, John Halliday, admired Thomas Carlyle very much and told us many stories about him.

The Hallidays loved books and education as most Scotch people do. I don't remember one thing about your gt-gt-G Halliday! And I believe I remember just one thing about gt. gt. Grandma H. That one thing is that she used to carry her shoes in her hand when she went calling so that they would not wear out too soon. (Maybe she knew it was good for her corns.)

Grandpa H. used to tell us that he loved his "bukes" so much that he used to hide where no one could find him at his home in Eccelfachen. (He pronounced "books" as tho spelled "byooks.") When he was past 90 yrs. old he still loved his books and always had one in his hands until his head nodded & he fell asleep. At that age he still quoted long parts of Shakespeare and Bobby Burns and, of course, the Bible.

After John Halliday learned to be a shoe-maker, he decided to live in England. He moved to the town of Penrith in Westmorland County. This county is close to Scotland. I believe it borders on Scotland.

Here John made shoes and violins! He played the bass viol in the Episcopal church and *there* he met Anne Kilner. (So you see it always pays to attend church!) . . .

Billy, I really believe that Anne Kilner's only brother lived at Swindale when grown-up and married. (I'll try to let you know later.)

THE KILNERS

Well now, we'll leave the Hallidays for a bit and consider the Kilners. They lived on an estate called "Field Head" about three miles from Penrith. This estate was entailed, which means that it must stay in the Kilner family generation after generation, until the laws of England are changed. It was given to a Kilner hundreds of years ago by an English king, as a reward for a good deed done to the king. It was handed down from father to son all these long years. Why then did William Kilner, Jr., not settle down at Field Head? Ah, *that* sad tale I'll tell you later if I have the courage, and feel it right to divulge family secrets. Your gt. grandma Halliday would not discuss that.

Well then, the foundations of this old house were made of rocks that had been used by the Romans when they occupied England way back how long ago I've forgotten. The stair-way in the house was made of these rocks and had been used so many years that deep hollows had been worn into the stairs. Because of this, Anne Kilner's father had them covered with oak. (Anne K. H. told me — "Anne Winters" — that they had a neighbor, Wm Winter, whose front steps were worn down the same way. I like to think that he may have been the ancestor of your "Winter" cousins. For that name was "Winter" until their ancestor came to the U.S.A. at the time of the War of 1812.)

Pardon the digression and we'll return to

    Field Head,
        Penrith,
            Morland,
                Westmorland,
                    England.

Well, you really should have known your gt. gt. Grandfather William Kilner. Was he ever strict with his family! And did he ever dress up! Knee britches and long white silk stockings and low shoes with silver buckles! When he got a hole in his stockings his daughters mended them and the mend must never show! . . .

Gt. gt. gramp K's wife was named Mary. She was very gentle and charming. She was always very busy about her household tasks and over-seeing the maids. Of course they had a scullery maid, besides the others. They went to market to hire their maids and hired them by the year. I believe they paid five pounds a year, which would be about fifty cents a week. Extra helpers came by the day and came so early and left so late that they had to carry lanterns. As I remember it, they were paid two shillings a day, or twenty-five cents for about fourteen hours work. (No wonder there were wars & rebellions.)

On the estate there were renters and as far as I've heard, your gt gt grp Kilner's chief work was to ride about and collect rent and over-see the workers. Naturally, our English ancestors were Episcopalians but some of the renters were Methodists. When Grp. Kilner went to collect the rent from one of these Methodist families, they said they could not pay, for they didn't have enought to eat. Grp did not believe them but sat and talked a while, and as they talked, a little boy of the family kept saying "tate noven" and pointing to the stove. The mother tried to make him stop talking but he kept pointing so Grp K. said "Open the oven door to satisfy him." The mother did not want to but at last had to, and sure enough there was a "tate" (cake) in the oven. Grp Kilner was very much shocked at such duplicity and the joke of it all, to me, was that Anne Kilner always tho't as long as she lived that Methodists could not be trusted.

(Don't you think, Billy, that it was rather sad if renters couldn't have any cake?)

I suppose the Kilners had many cows as they made many tubs of cheese. These were kept in a milk house that had a spring of water running thru it — or rather the spring brot the water in and it flowed out as a stream. As the house was made of rocks and set low in the ground it stayed cool all the time. (I believe that it seldom gets very hot in England. At least when they kill poultry to eat, it does not have to be kept on ice but simply hangs in the meat house.)

The Kilners had many geese that were driven away to pasture as we in the U.S. take sheep out to feed.

They had very fine food in great quantities but they were very careful about their eating. They never had butter and meat at the same meal.

There was a separate kitchen for all of the hired men and women. Also, the children were not allowed to eat with their parents until they learned correct table manners.

And *then*, believe it or not, the grown-ups *sat* at the table and the children stood up!

These people you see believed in hardening their children

> "Cast the bantling on the rock —
> Nurtured by the wind and frost,
> Power and speed be hands and feet."

That seemed to be their idea in bring[ing] up children. We, here, could never have been so severe. (I'll tell you some stories about that stern upbringing in another chapter.)

William and Mary Kilner had five children, the one son William, Jr., and of course four daughters. I am not sure whether Wm Jr. was the eldest child or not, but in any case he was the only son and so in line to inherit the property.

The daughters were in this order: Mary, Elizabeth, Anne, and Isabella. Of all the children, Anne was her father's favorite for the strange reason that she was not afraid of him and told him what she thot.

(This no[te] written under great difficulties.)

APPENDIX 2. The Architecture of a Craftsman Bungalow

When Mervin V. Palmer, a Flandreau, South Dakota, contractor-builder,[1] built my parents' house in 1919, the *Pipestone Leader* noted that "William Morgan has a foundation laid and dimension material on the grounds to start building his 34 × 42' story and one half, 11 room semi-bungalow on south Anna [now Third Avenue]. . . . Mr. and Mrs. Morgan have been for several months planning their ideal new home, and its cost was in the neighborhood of $12,000."[2]

The house is a Craftsman bungalow, inspired by "The Westly," a mail-order, prefabricated structure designed by Sears, Roebuck and Company.[3] Like "The Westly," the Morgan house has a gabled roof with deep, bracketed overhangs, a gabled dormer, and a symmetrical window arrangement. The interior plan also parallels the Sears house: a central hall, a comparable room arrangement and room use, a beveled-glass entry door, and an oak buffet.

The exterior of the Morgan house combines some of the best symmetrical and organic features found in Craftsman bungalows. The symmetry of the front (east) facade is marked by a central porch, a doorway with flanking sidelights, a balanced fenestration, and an axial gabled dormer. Several organic elements soften this rather rigid symmetry: large, light-screen-type windowpanes; frosted glass, incised with plant designs, in the entrance door and sidelights; and an Oriental-style porch with projecting roof, battered columns, and post-and-beam construction. In the early twenties, before ice buildup forced their removal, the porch was flanked by rounded steps, designed to resemble flowing water.

The interior design also carries through the interplay of the symmetrical and the organic. Although floor plans on both levels follow the Georgian ideal of a central hall with flanking rooms, an attempt was made to break up this symmetry by curving the downstairs hall and creating nooks and angles in the kitchen. While the central-hall plan provides efficient circulation, the natural spatial flow is more the result of the size and the placement of windows. Windows in the living room, sun parlor, and dining room, as well as the glass doors with trellis-shaped mullions that connect these rooms, provide large amounts of light from the east and the south. A glass-enclosed mudroom/porch on the south allows a sunny entrance into an otherwise dark kitchen. Some sixty-seven individual openings, not counting basement windows, illuminate the house.[4]

Another important organic element is the way wood is used. Honey-colored oak woodwork and oak and maple flooring appear throughout the house. The frame is built from southern pine, which Bill Forman, the present owner, says is "so hard you can't drive a nail into it." My brother Stan remembers that to prevent splitting, carpenters first soaked finishing nails in beeswax before driving them into the oak trim. The narrow clapboarding is original and of such high quality that it has been painted only three times. A wide stairwell, lighted at landing level with a large window, beveled glass in the major rooms, hand-stenciled wall designs, a built-in buffet, and glass bookcases underscore the builder's and clients' strong awareness of organic design. Although no indirect lighting is featured, a built-in ironing board, clothes chute, broom closets, and a mopboard-hidden vacuum system reveal the builder's knowledge of some of the practical elements used by progressive architects.

All these features make the Morgan home, to use Alan Gowans's term, a "comfortable house." Designed to hold a family of six, the house, from 1919 to 1936, served that purpose well. When the last sibling left home, the house sheltered only two people, and for six or seven of those years, it was cut up into three apartments. My mother lived alone from 1951 until her death in 1964. After her son-in-law restored the house in 1966, Bill and Courtenay have lived there ever since. To this day, 310 attracts their children, grandchildren, and Morgan relatives who return for a visit and consider the house a family seat much as a lord's clan would consider the manor.

APPENDIX 3.

Gen. George J. Stannard, Forgotten Hero of the Civil War

"Glory to God! Glory to God!" [General] Doubleday shouted, swinging his hat in approval as he watched from [Cemetery Ridge]. "See the Vermonters go it!"
— Shelby Foote, *The Civil War*

"As we marched over that fatal field never was I more confident of victory. But when I saw that Damn Vermont Colonel [*sic*] on foot, hat off, sword swinging in air in front of his men and cheering them on upon our flank, I knew we were doomed."
— Gary Gallagher, *Fighting for the Confederacy*

George Jerrison Stannard, the brigadier general praised by Union general Abner Doubleday and cursed by a Confederate colonel captured at Gettysburg, was born in East Georgia, Franklin County, Vermont, October 20, 1820. As a young man, he worked on his family's farm and taught school during winters. In 1850, he married Emily Clark, to whom three children were born. Before the Civil War, Stannard owned and managed a foundry in nearby St. Albans, Vermont.[1]

Stannard's military career began at age seventeen when, as a member of the state militia, he served as his company's first sergeant. In 1856, as the unit's first lieutenant, he organized an independent company of militia called the Ransom Guard. When war broke out, Stannard was the first Vermonter to answer Lincoln's call for troops.[2] In June 1861, he was promoted to lieutenant colonel of the Second Vermont Infantry Regiment and was cited for bravery at Bull Run. In May 1862, as colonel of the Ninth Vermont Regiment, Stannard returned to Vermont to recruit and drill troops whom he took to the Shenandoah Valley to resist Lee's advance into Maryland.[3]

On September 15, 1862, Stannard's regiment, among others, was forced to surrender to Stonewall Jackson at Harpers Ferry. Stannard, who adamantly opposed surrender without a fight, refused to sign paroles for himself or his troops until so ordered by a higher-ranking officer. According to Stannard's biographer, Col. Albert Clarke, Stannard begged for permission to take and hold a height or to cut his way out.[4]

Following the surrender that proved to be inevitable, Stonewall Jackson rode up to the Ninth Vermont and said, "Boys, don't feel bad. You could not help it. It was just as God willed it." At that point a member of Jackson's staff asked Stannard if he was carrying whiskey. When Stannard handed the officer his flask, the Confederate poured himself a drink and said, "Colonel, here is to the health of the Southern Confederacy." Horrified by this breach of military etiquette, Stannard responded, "To ask and accept a courtesy of a prisoner and then insult him is an act that an honorable soldier would scorn." Stannard then was quoted as saying:

> "Jackson turned on his staff officer and gave him a severe scolding, saying the repetition of such an insult to a prisoner would cost him his place. Then turning to me, General Jackson apologized for the conduct of his officer, saying that it was an exceptional act of insolence on the part of a young and reckless man. And, bowing gravely, the famous Confederate captain rode away."[5]

Several months later, Stannard was exchanged, and upon his return to service, he was promoted to brigadier general and placed in command of recruits assigned to the defense of Washington, D.C.

Stannard's troops next saw action during the summer of 1863. On the evening of July 1, as Union troops moved toward Gettysburg, Stannard's brigade, after "an exhausting seven-day march plagued by daily rains and soggy roads,"[6] joined Doubleday's First Corps, Army of the Potomac. On July 2, the brigade was massed on the south edge of Cemetery Hill, where Stannard's soldiers could see the action taking place on Little Round Top, Devil's Den, the Wheat Field, and the Peach Orchard. At sunset, Stannard was ordered forward to close a gap in the Union line where Confederates had just captured two Union batteries. Moving into position, Stannard's troops closed the line and recovered the guns. Nightfall found the Vermont brigade south of the Angle on Cemetery Ridge.[7]

Stannard's position on Cemetery Ridge proved to be crucial to the success of the following day's battle. As Pickett's men moved across the field toward the Union defenses, Union general Alexander Hays's men on the far north end of the ridge wheeled left, enveloping the advancing left flank of Pettigrew's and Trimble's Confederate divisions. At about the same time, Stannard moved his three regiments one hundred yards forward, where they fortified a small knoll. When the Vermonters' position left Gen. James Kemper's advancing Confederate brigade exposed, Stannard ordered his regiments northward, rolling up Kemper's right flank.[8]

The day before, veteran troops had scorned the nine hundred Vermont nine-month recruits ("nine monthlings hatched from $200 bounty eggs") who had just completed easy duty near Washington and who were now nearing completion of their service. According to historian George R. Stewart, "Except for one or two insignificant skirmishes with Stuart's cavalry, [the Vermonters] had heard no bullets until July 2. Then they had suddenly found themselves opposed to an advancing line. Scarcely knowing what they were doing, they had charged, had halted the Confederates, driven them back, and taken heavy casualties."[9] According to historian Shelby Foote, the Vermonters were determined to show their ability before going home:

> Now the opportunity was at hand. Company by company, they opened fire as they wheeled into line, blasting the rebel flank, and as they delivered their murderous volleys they continued to move northward, closing the range until their officers were able to add the fire of their revolvers to the weight of metal thrown into the writhing mass of graybacks. "Glory to God! Glory to God!" Doubleday shouted, swinging his hat in approval as he watched from up the slope. "See the Vermonters go it!"[10]

With success at hand, Stannard recalled his troops. At the moment of victory, however, a piece of shrapnel penetrated his right thigh. Although injured, Stannard refused to leave the field until his wounded men had been carried to safety and fresh troops had arrived to relieve his exhausted brigade. Clarke wrote: "I remember how, with [field]glass in one hand and hat in the other, [Stannard] emphasized his orders by gestures and sturdily faced the destructive fire without showing the least concern. Although he knew we were but atoms in a tremendous convulsion, somehow we all felt that he would make the most of us, and he did."[11]

Following the battle, while nursing his unhealed wound, Stannard commanded several forts in New York harbor. In May 1864, he was reassigned to the Army of the Potomac, in which he commanded a brigade under a fellow Vermonter, Maj. Gen. William F. Smith. A month later at Cold Harbor, Virginia, "Stannard made three gallant and desperate charges. Twice he nearly reached the breastworks in front; but the raking fire from both flanks was too deadly to be endured, and he relinquished the attempt."[12] During this attack, every man in his staff was killed or wounded, and Stannard was wounded twice in the thigh. While advancing on Petersburg in July, Stannard was again painfully wounded when one of his own officers accidentally fired his pistol, hitting the general's finger.[13]

After a short furlough, Stannard returned to the front. On September 29, the Eighteenth Corps moved north of the James River, where Stannard was ordered to capture Fort Harrison, a bastion located south of Richmond. Hoping to rest his exhausted troops, Stannard asked General Grant to relieve his command, a request to which Grant replied, "It is very essential that we take this fort and I know you will do it."[14] Fort Harrison lay fourteen hundred yards across an open field and was heavily fortified. After leading his troops across the field, Stannard was able to capture the fort's northeast angle but at a loss of all his brigade commanders, four regimental commanders, and 18 percent of his men.[15] Securing the rear of the fort, Stannard's troops repulsed three assaults by the reinforced Confederates. While pacing a parapet, sword and hat in either hand, Stannard sustained his fifth and most serious wound of the war, resulting in the amputation of his right arm at the shoulder. An unnamed officer wrote: "I have often said that General Stannard held Fort Harrison against desperate odds of men fighting under the inspiration of Lee's own presence, by the sheer force of personal character. And there was not another division or another general of the Army of the James that could have done it. He was an army in himself in such supreme moments."[16] For his service at Fort Harrison, Stannard was brevetted major general of volunteers on October 28, 1864. In December, Stannard was transferred to St. Albans to serve garrison duty following the Confederate raid on his hometown.[17]

Stannard's courage was matched by his compassion. When he assumed command of a unit formerly headed by a West Pointer, Stannard found that his predecessor had ordered a man tied up by his thumbs because he had not saluted an officer. When the prisoner was brought before Stannard, the general quietly talked to him "as though both had come from the same neighborhood," and the man was released. At Gettysburg, a lieutenant was arrested for getting water for his troops from a guarded well. When the lieutenant pleaded with Stannard to allow him to fight rather than spend time in jail, the court-martial was dropped.[18]

Very little is known about Stannard's postwar career. According to his pension records, Stannard suffered years of debilitating pain from his multiple wounds.[19] In 1866, after retiring from active duty, he was assigned to the Freedman's Bureau at Baltimore and later accepted an appointment as collector of customs in Burlington, Vermont. From 1881 until his death in 1886, the former general was doorkeeper of the U.S. House of Representatives.[20]

"Fifteen Months on a North Dakota Claim"

The following reminiscence was written by Marilla Holliday Wauchope, daughter of William Holliday, when Marilla was in her seventies (1948).

In 1862 Congress passed the first Homestead Law whereby a man or woman, twenty one years of age or over, could acquire one hundred and sixty acres of land for a farm without capital. Requirements for "taking up a claim" consisted in living on the land for at least fourteen months and cultivating it.

By 1900 there were few good claims left in the United States barring Alaska, and claim holders tried to obtain additional acreage by having friends lend their names as homesteaders on adjoining land. When such manipulations were exposed the land had to be surrendered, and due to such a circumstance I was able to take up a claim to land in North Dakota in 1907. Friends had given glowing accounts of living on a claim and my imagination painted an exciting and adventurous picture for me. I had, no doubt, inherited some of the pioneering spirit of my grandfather [Joseph Woods Hancock], who with his wife and infant daughter came to the middle east of Minnesota to teach and live among the Dakota Indians. It was my grandfather who named what became the town of Red Wing in honor of Red Wing, the Indian Chief.

When a letter came from Mr. Pierson, a lawyer in North Dakota, telling me that land was available 22 miles from the Canadian border I grasped the opportunity with great expectations. It was required that one live on the land for two summers, cultivating ten acres and paying a small sum of money at the end of fourteen months. I was thrilled at the prospect of having one hundred and sixty acres of land all my own. My family did not receive my decision with like enthusiasm; my brother was convinced that I was the last person on earth to live alone, miles from civilization or another human being. His skepticism made me all the more determined to try or die. My father's willing acceptance of my plans was the only encouragement I received.

It was in April 1907 when after months of planning I was ready to start out for the promised land, accompanied by my father. We left by train for Bowbells, N.D., which was sixteen miles from the site of my claim. When we arrived the ground was covered with snow, and more was falling. We were held up in Bowbells for several days. I hired a local young man by the name of Wesley Johnson to build my shack. After the snowstorm subsided, Wesley set out to break trail with a team of horses and a sleigh laden with lumber, boxes and some pieces of furniture. My father and I followed the next day in another sleigh. It was a bitterly cold day. I pulled the robes about me and felt aglow. This was the real beginning of my adventure; the mere thought of it should keep me warm. But no adventure without hardship. It came when one of the two horses broke through the ice on the trail and began some wild plunging. While my father wrestled with the reins I jumped out, grabbed the bridle of the frightened animal and led the sleigh to firmer ground. Not until then had I paid any attention to my own frozen feet and the wet clothing which was hanging from the waist like stiff boards, for during the rescue operations I had slipped into the hole of icy water into which the horse had stumbled. Shivering I slid under the robes in the sleigh with somewhat cooled spirits. Four miles along the trail we were supposed to find a little store where I would be able to thaw out. Those four miles were the longest four miles in my life. When we finally reached the store I was certain that never before did a country store potbellied stove give so much comfort to any human being as this one in the plains of North Dakota gave to me.

As soon as I was dry we continued our trip and followed the tracks Wesley Johnson had made. It was already dark when we reached the Pierson shack, our temporary abode, where we found Wesley. The roaring fire in the small stove did its best to warm us shivering homesteaders, but there were just too many cracks in the walls. With our clothes and heavy coats we went to sleep, at least we tried to sleep, on the hard unfriendly cots. We welcomed the morning light and enjoyed hot coffee, flapjacks and eggs.

My father and Wesley were getting ready to build my shack on top of a hill which sloped gently down to a lake shaped like an hourglass. While the men worked I took a look around. The land was flat, interrupted here and there by rolling hills. I had a far view from my little hill. Here and there and well distanced were some other shacks. Their snow-covered roofs blended into the white landscape; only walls swept clean by the wind and small windows protected by the roof gave them away as dwellings. Even in this vast desolate whiteness I could sense beauty and feel exhilaration because it was to be my land and my home. So, undismayed by physical discomforts, I too set to work. I helped Wesley shingle the roof with my father's fur coat over my own heavy coat. I looked like a bear rolling back and forth over the roof challenging Wesley to beat me. He was a faster talker than worker, but we finished shingling the roof in good time as a 16 × 16 foot room did not present much of a problem. Soon my father was able to install the two-lid laundry stove which had a drum oven in the stove pipe. Lighting the first fire in it became a ceremonious event of great significance. For the first time in four days we felt warm and were soon shedding layers of clothing. We lost no time in bringing our few belongings over from the Pierson shack and bid goodbye to Wesley who was moving on to his claim.

The following days were spent in decorating the interior. After the two bedframes were completed we went to pick bushels of cattails at a nearby pond. We shelled out the fluff and stuffed it into mattress covers and were delighted with our warm and comfortable mattresses. The inside walls were then covered with pink building paper. To complete the decor I sewed bedspreads, window curtains, hangings for a simulated closet, curtains for cupboards made from boxes, and a table cover. The yards and yards of cretonne of blue background with pink roses which I had purchased in Red Wing, Minnesota, made the room look very cheerful. There was suddenly an air of gaiety and summer inside. To complete the luxury I had one rocker, two straight chairs, and a table. The neighbors approvingly called my shack "the palace." Father decided that the palace wasn't complete without a kitchen, and no sooner said than he began to work on the foundation. He laid the floor and put up some "two by fours" then wisely left the rest for me to finish. The time of his departure had come and it was a sad day when he left. His farewell gift was the spring which he discovered and cleaned out before he left so that I was provided with good drinking water.

Building the kitchen kept me busy from morning till night and I was grateful to my father for providing me with a project which left little time to feel lonesome. The kitchen was not exactly built according to Hoyle. The walls took on a gory appearance as I impartially sawed and pounded fingers as well as boards. I felt very proud of myself when the walls were up, the roof completed, and a sliding window put in, and then I discovered to my dismay that I had made no provision to enter the "palace" except by crawling through a window. This oversight was corrected by sawing through the wall from the living room, and no carpenter was ever so proud of his work as I was of that kitchen.

After completion of this project another very challenging task presented itself in the persons of Ruth and Donald Wallace whose tutoring I promised to undertake in return for errands in town for vegetables, milk, butter and eggs. The Wallaces were the closest neighbors — living only two miles from me. When the weather was too stormy for the children to walk home they stayed overnight. They were the only visitors for a long while until one day a heavily bearded man came walking over the hill. I had been working outdoors when he approached and frightened me, for his appearance was far from reassuring. It was Mr. Knapp who lived on the other side of the lake and apparently knew everyone in this part of North Dakota. Sitting on the rock just outside my door he regaled me with stories about the people and every sentence was spiced with profanity. However, my first impression betrayed his true nature, later he proved to be a kind neighbor.

In July my father came back and brought with him my friend, Adelaide Apfeld, from St. Paul, Minnesota. On the evening of their arrival a terrible windstorm raged and continued all night. I walked the floor and kept feeling the walls bulging in and out and knew that we were all going to be blown away. Whenever I called to my father, who was supposed to be asleep in the kitchen, he answered cheerfully, but later he confessed that he was frightened, himself, for he did not think my carpenter work would be able to withstand the strain of such wrath of nature. And if the kitchen went, the rest of the structure would go with it. Adelaide, exhausted from her trip, would have slept through it all had it not been for my trying to keep her alerted. About midnight there was a loud knock at the door. Frightened and with a feeling of ill foreboding I opened the door just a crack and holding on with all my might against the wind I looked into the darkness but saw nothing. Then I heard Mrs. Pierson's voice from below. She and her son had crawled on hands and knees and finally reached my door exhausted and shaken not daring to stand up lest the wind blow them away from the haven of safety. The Pierson shack did not withstand the storm, and hearing what happened to our neighbors increased our anxiety. Our own heavy heartbeats mingled with the howling and whistling, the creaking and rattling. The hours until daybreak were filled with tensions. Then suddenly there was silence, a deep, wonderful, relaxing silence as if the wind itself had felt the need for peace and quietude. Later in the day we went over to the Pierson shack and found it ten feet off its foundation. With an apparent sense of humor, at least this is the way we perceived it, the storm had mixed several dozen eggs with a bottle of bluing and had left a big blue green and violet palette on the kitchen floor. The Piersons went back to their home in town and never returned, not even for an occasional weekend.

During Adelaide's month-long visit we had another bout with the weatherman. A hailstorm riddled the tar paper on the kitchen roof resulting in my losing faith in tar paper after the two storms. And, expert that I had become, I showed Adelaide how to shingle a roof. I also found a good hiking companion in Adelaide and we explored the countryside together. When her visit came to an end I felt very sad to see her go. After her departure Ruth and Donald Wallace returned for their lessons and we resumed our studies in earnest.

It was September now. The rest of the summer had gone by uneventfully, only mailday remained a weekly event of significance. Mail was brought in once a week, but we had to call for it five miles away. This walk seemed never long and I was looking forward to it eagerly. I learned from Miss Linwell, the school teacher, to wade across the narrows of the lake, later the other homesteaders filled the narrows with rock, and we were able to walk across dry shod. One day I found the path across the lake washed away, but on my return our self-appointed road committee had restored it. I was glad I did not have to carry my heavy walking shoes in addition to an armful of letters, newspapers and magazines. Halfway across the narrows a rock slipped from underneath my foot and I measured my length in cold water, spilling my precious load. I rescued the water-soaked mail and resumed walking the last half mile home, shivering and dripping. By the time I reached my door I was perfectly dry and suffered no ill effects from this unanticipated bath.

Maildays seem to have been the occasions for excitement other than hearing from the outside world. It was a foggy day when Ruth, who had been staying with me, and I started out for the mail. I was not concerned about the fog for I knew these five miles so well I was certain I could walk them blindfolded, but then I had not experienced before such thick impenetrable fog, and it wasn't long before I realized I had lost my bearing. We must have been walking in circles and I became panic stricken at the thought of my responsibility for Ruth. Lost on the North Dakota prairie! I saw us forlorn and shivering, spending the cold night wandering, followed by packs of roaming coyotes whose weird laughterlike howling sent chills through my bones even when in the safety of my shack. How soon would the fog lift? What should one do in such an emergency? Fear froze all channels of clear thinking. Suddenly we heard footsteps and a man's voice. Never will I forget the feeling of relief! The owner of that voice lived in a shack nearby. He led us safely to my shack which at the moment really looked like a palace to me.

My father came again on the first of October and I was expecting to go home with him for the winter. However, he informed me that the law now demanded a continual residence of fourteen months else it meant giving up the claim. He thought I should not stay, but I finally convinced him that I could manage alright for the winter months. In order to help me prepare for the cold weather he borrowed a plow and a horse, plowed up sod and piled it four feet high around the outside walls. Untold times during the bitterly cold days later in the season I thanked him for this wise precaution. Now, even at 40 degrees below zero, which was not an unusual temperature, it took only a few minutes to heat up the place.

Father had dug a cellar of about four cubic feet under the kitchen floor where I could keep food from freezing. We also gathered buckbrush for kindling which we piled up in the kitchen next to a big heap of coal from town. There was little room left, but to have an abundance of fuel was comforting.

On the morning before my father's departure, we noticed a long line of smoke several miles away steadily coming nearer. Father lost no time plowing furrows around the shack; then the smoke seemed to die down and we went inside to eat dinner. Suddenly out of nowhere a man came rushing in calling excitedly: "The wind has changed, the fire is coming this way very fast." We could see it leap forward with unbelievable speed, flames shooting 7–8 feet up into the air. Men were hauling barrels of water to fight the blaze. The fire was halted at the furrows father had plowed just a few rods from the shack. These furrows were the first lines of resistance which proved effective, and the fire was soon brought under control and my homestead was saved.

During the winter months Mr. Knapp brought my mail. I was no longer afraid of him although his bearded appearance and his manner of speech had not changed. One Sunday I met Matt from Bowbells at the Wallaces who had invited both of us for dinner. Matt took me home with his lovely sleigh and beautiful team of horses. Next day the children told me that Matt had asked to board with the Wallaces all winter. I could not help feeling somewhat apprehensive and asked the children never to let him come over alone to see me. The youngsters kept their promise until one day when Matt managed to get away from them unnoticed. I was sorting things in my makeshift cellar and when I stuck my head up there was Matt standing at the door. I was startled and amused at the same time thinking of the picture I must present with my head and shoulders sticking up above the kitchen floor, like a Jack in the Box. Matt seemed pleased that he succeeded in getting away from Ruth and Donald. My welcome was not very cordial; I let dinnertime pass by and it became quite evident that I had no intention to invite him for a meal. He finally left. He made a remark to the Wallaces about me to the effect that if I would only treat a man the way I treated my cat, I would be wonderful. (I have indeed a great fondness for these creatures.) Matt did not stay for the winter; he packed up and went back to town.

One evening Wesley Johnson showed up. Lonely winter days and a bright moonlight brought him over from his claim to ask if I would go coasting with him on scoop shovels. Coasting was fun; having been raised in Minnesota I was fond of all winter sports, but coasting on scoop shovels was something new. The children were staying with me that night and were at once very enthusiastic about the idea. I took my scoop shovel and one smaller one and up we went on the little hill. It was light outside, the bright moonlight was reflected by a hard glistening snow cover. We certainly did not coast the usual way. We sat on the shovel facing the handle and with hands and feet wrapped around the handle we started down-hill. We whirled, we slid, we went sidewise and backward, we slipped off and climbed on again until we reached the bottom of the hill. What fun this was! I doubt there has ever been so much laughter on this hill before or since.

Happy hours like these made up for many lonely nights when howling coyotes seemed to be the only living things in North Dakota. I would go to bed with my head covered to keep out the eerie high-pitched howling of these pitiful creatures that roamed the countryside in desperate search for food. And there were days when I was in great need for someone's helping hands, like on the morning when my stove pipe fell down as I was kindling the fire. It was about 12 feet to where the pipe went through the roof. I had no ladder. It was very cold and stories went through my mind of people freezing to death on their claims. In desperation I put the table over the stove and a chair on the top of the table, but I couldn't begin to reach high enough. I put several lengths of stove pipe together and tried to maneuver it into the hole in the roof. I did not dare give up and tried it again and again. My hands were numb with cold, they didn't seem to belong to me, and my arms and shoulders were sore and tired. With one last desperate effort the pipe slipped through the hole.

To my surprise new neighbors arrived around Christmas time, Mr. and Mrs. White and their two daughters. Their claim adjoined mine. Mr. White was full of fun and liked to tease. One day he appeared out of nowhere in front of my window where I was sitting. I was so startled that I slid to the floor. Mr. White apologized and said: "Wesley told me that you are a good Christian girl and I thought a Christian wasn't afraid of anything." "Oh yes," I replied, "a Christian is always afraid of the devil."

Queer tales reached my ear about the schoolteacher, Miss Linwell. It was said that she pointed a loaded revolver at the children to impress them with her authority. The trustees acted quickly and closed the school. The next day Miss Linwell came to visit me, carrying the basket in which she was supposed to keep her revolver. She looked so lonely, I did not have the heart to let her go home and asked her to spend the night with me. I was troubled and worried and wondering whether the revolver story was true and if she had the revolver with her what she might do.

Fortunately it was about time for Miss Linwell to "prove up" on her claim. She asked Mr. White and me to be her witnesses to confirm before a commissioner that she had complied with the law regarding her time of residence on the land. Mr. White had told her that he was delighted to be her witness and that, of course, he expected her to treat him to some drinks in return. She was absolutely aghast! Poor Miss Linwell, she did not know that Mr. White himself was a staunch temperance man and a great teaser. She gave him a classic temperance lecture, much to his delight. Then her big day came and we went with her to the land office in Kenmare. After her claim to the land was duly recorded and legalized, Miss Linwell treated us to a dinner at the best hotel in town. Mr. White couldn't resist teasing and said: "Miss Linwell you have entertained us most graciously, some good wine now would make this day complete." Miss Linwell drew her lips tight, she looked angry and her fists hit the table as she exclaimed: "The best fresh fruit in town, but not a drop to drink." We were ready to drop through the floor as other guests present stared at us and Mr. White hastened to tell her that he was only joking. North Dakota was a dry state and the mention of alcoholic beverages was akin to deathly sin, and temptation lurked very near, only 22 miles at the Canadian border. Surely it couldn't have been people from North Dakota who threw empty whisky bottles across the border, perhaps it was Satan himself who did it in a teasing mood. I had no difficulty picking up an empty bottle the label of which was still like new. I kept the bottle with a definite purpose in mind.

About three months after we accompanied Miss Linwell, my own claim had to be "proved up." It was also to be my last day on the claim. Father had arrived earlier to help me pack and everything was ready. Mr. White was one of my witnesses and we went through the same procedure in Kenmare, establishing legal possession, celebrating the occasion with a dinner at the hotel and then, instead of going back to the shack, proceeded to the depot to take the afternoon train home to Minnesota. I found many of my neighbors waiting at the station to bid us farewell. With due ceremony I handed Mr. White my surprise package which contained the whisky bottle filled with tea that truly looked like what the label claimed: the best Old English Whisky. Mr. White looked at it with suspicion then broke the seal, opened it and took a good deep sniff like a connoisseur. He urged the neighbors and friends to share in a farewell toast for us with him, and the more he insisted the harder the good people resisted. Some had caught on but did not give the joke away. Attracted by the laughing and joking, the sheriff arrived at the scene, and filled with the importance of his position, he was ready to enforce the law. By this time most had recognized the contents of the bottle and greeted his efforts with hilarious laughter. The merrier and louder the laughter, the angrier the sheriff became and he was going to arrest every one of us. My father finally told him to smell the bottle. His dignity crushed and feeling hurt he withdrew in a hurry. There was no time for sadness as the train pulled in and we departed. The laughing and shouting of good wishes by the many good friends I had found were long lingering in my ears as the train sped homeward.

NOTES

Introduction

1. "John Halliday," in Philip Dunaway and Mel Evans, eds., *A Treasury of the World's Great Diaries* (New York: Doubleday, 1957), 43–49. The original journal is owned by Ellen Holliday, Mt. Kisco, New York. "GAR Convention Journal," Warrington B. Brown, August 1924, unpublished. Possession of author. As a young woman, my mother was an enthusiastic diarist. Sadly, she burned all except one of her diaries.

2. Catherine Hanf Noren, *The Camera of My Family* (New York: Knopf, 1976); Dorothy Redford, *Somerset Homecoming* (New York: Doubleday, 1988).

3. Henry Glassie, "The Wedderspoon Farm," *New York Folklife Quarterly* 22, no. 3 (September 1966): 165–87. This essay was particularly useful as a guide to my own fieldwork. Howard Wight Marshall, *Folk Architecture in Little Dixie: A Regional Culture in Missouri* (Columbia: University of Missouri Press, 1981).

4. The Flowerdew research is contained in James Deetz, *Flowerdew Hundred: The Archaeology of a Virginia Plantation, 1619–1864* (Charlottesville: University Press of Virginia, 1993).

5. Wright Morris, *The Inhabitants* (New York: Da Capo, 1972), n.p., my emphasis.

1. The Spaces and Places of My Childhood

1. Courtenay Morgan-Forman, "Courtenay's History," unpublished memoir, May 1993, 5. Mother once told me *she* knew by her second month that she was pregnant. I was thrilled when my brothers once told me my father knew my mother was carrying a child.

2. Homer and Langley Collyer were eccentric brothers who lived in a three-story Harlem mansion from 1909 until their deaths in 1947. Although wealthy and educated, the brothers lived for years without gas, electricity, water, or sewage. After they died, authorities discovered that the mansion was honeycombed with tunnels made of garbage, cardboard crates, and bundles of newspapers. Sons of Herman L. Collyer, a

New York gynecologist, Homer was an admiralty lawyer and Langley a concert pianist. Harold Faber, "Homer Collyer, Harlem Recluse, Found Dead at 70," *New York Times*, March 22, 1947.

3. Loran (Bud) Morgan, letter to the author, August 3, 1992.

4. Walter Morgan made his famous jump on October 11, 1948, in Fosston, Minnesota. Two thousand spectators, including his wife and six children, watched Walter free fall for some distance before pulling the ripcord. After leaving the plane and making a complete somersault, Walter was quoted as saying, "Falling through the air was so pleasant I just decided not to pull the cord for a while." It was believed at the time that Walter was the oldest person ever to make a parachute jump. "Fosston Farmer, 76, Jumps 1,800 Feet," *Minneapolis Morning Tribune*, October 12, 1948.

5. There were 1.5 million spotters during World War II. The circular plane spotter's guide is shown in *This Fabulous Century, 1940–1950* (New York: Time-Life Books, 1969), 156.

6. "Roger Dibble Circles City in Army Plane," *Pipestone County Star*, August 10, 1944.

7. The victory garden concept was initiated in December 1941 by the secretary of agriculture, Claude R. Wickard. By 1943, 20.5 million garden plots were in cultivation (*This Fabulous Century*, 158).

8. Evelyn Fairbanks's memoir of life in St. Paul includes a four-page description of the terrors of lighting a furnace in the dark cavern of a Minnesota basement. Fairbanks writes: "It wasn't just the near-empty coal bin that held terror, for even when there was plenty of coal, the big empty space behind the furnace and on the other side of the basement seemed to be full of things that made tiny noises when the rest of the house was so quiet. I kept dropping coal on the floor that I had to pick up, all the while being watched by those things in the shadows. I wanted to cry, but that would have made too much noise, and I wouldn't hear the things; and besides, Mama would get mad if I cried" (Evelyn Fairbanks, *Days of Rondo* [St. Paul: Minnesota Historical Society Press, 1990], 16).

My brother Alan challenges my view of the basement: "This matter of the scary basement really invites a vast comparison, for I think we three older brothers loved it. I had a so-called gymnasium down there. And the fact that the house was once heated with coal was most fascinating. Two rooms on the south side held coal. Now and then a delivery man would bring us a fresh supply. It would be put in those two rooms when we had raised the windows and a metal slide was inserted into them. 'Stoking' the furnace was also great fun" (Alan Morgan, letter to the author, October 19, 1994).

9. Henry P. Fischer, a Canadian physician, discovered sulfur springs in nearby Carver County and established Mudcura in 1908. According to its charter, Mudcura provided treatment "especially [for] those suffering from rheumatism and skin, kidney, and nerve diseases" (Patricia Engelmann, "The Tradition of Healing Water," unpublished essay, American Studies Program, St. Cloud State University, 1992, 4). The sanatorium closed in 1956.

2. My Journey to Field Head, England

1. "John Halliday," 43.

2. William T. Morgan, Kilner genealogy files, 1984–1996.

3. Anne Winters, letter to the author, April 17, 1961. When Anne's son Warrington visited Field Head in 1945, he learned that the farm belonged to a Charles Baker-Courtenay. In 1971, renters told Warrington's daughter Anne Williamson that William Kilner lost the estate to a Lord Courtenay and that Courtenay's sister had married a man named Charles Baker, who gained control of Field Head by changing his name to Baker-Courtenay. George Harrison's father, Stanley, purchased Field Head from Baker-Courtenay for 17,000 pounds in 1969.

4. Dorothy Smith, letter to the author, October 1, 1987.

5. Dorothy Smith, research notes from the Great Strickland, Glenridding, and Patterdale census returns, October 1, 1987. Mrs. Smith also had access to the Greenside Mine paybook, in which William's wages are recorded. In 1989, David Fallowfield sifted through hundreds of land deeds related to Field Head without finding new evidence concerning the loss of the farm (David Fallowfield, letter to the author, June 15, 1989). A story written by Fallowfield, "Ancestor Hears Tale of Family Farm 'Lost in Card Game,'" in the *Cumberland and Westmorland Herald* on July 8, 1989, records a visit to Field Head that David, my son, Bill, and I made in 1988.

3. My Journey to Ecclefechan, Scotland

1. Anne Winters, letter to the author, April 17, 1961.

2. Morland census records, compiled by Robert Twaits, Great Strickland, England.

3. Travel books and literary histories mention Ecclefechan (though generally without enthusiasm) because of its connection to Thomas Carlyle. During my stay I boarded in a house built by Carlyle's father. Carlyle's birthplace, across the street, was also built by members of the Carlyle family. (Anne wrote that John Halliday admired Carlyle and often told stories about him.) A typical account notes the "straggling street[s] of the rude village" and "the dreary surroundings of this hard and rough village" (Theodore F. Wolfe, *A Literary Pilgrimage among the Haunts of Famous British Authors* [Philadelphia: J. B. Lippincott, 1897], 162). While living in England, I discovered that local comedians used the sound of the word "Ecclefechan"—with the emphasis on *fech*—as a source of bawdy humor. People would say to me, "Why would anyone want to visit Ecclefechan?"

4. Carlisle and Solway Firth, sheet 85, Landranger Series of Great Britain, 1976.

5. Plan of the Estate of Luce, map (Edinburgh: McFarlane, ca. 1830). This rare map is owned by Drew Clark, Dumfries, Scotland.

6. *Annan Parish Censuses, 1801–1821*, n.s. 4 (Edinburgh: Scottish Record Society, 1975). The 1801 census shows thirty-eight people residing at Brownmoor. General Dirom, his wife, two sons, five daughters, and four male and eight female servants are listed as living at nearby Mount Annan.

7. William Crawford & Son, Map of Dumfrieshire, sheet 6, part 4, SE (Edinburgh: John Thomson, 1828).

8. An early directory lists five boot- and shoemakers and four clogmakers in Ecclefechan and surrounding areas (*Royal National Commercial Directory and Topography of Scotland* [London: Isaac Slater, 1852], 396–97). Perhaps John Halliday moved to England to find a less competitive environment.

4. The Hallidays' Journey to America

1. "John Halliday," 43–49. John Halliday's great-grandson Warrington Winters used the original journal for the selections that appear in the Doubleday anthology. The published excerpts begin on August 28, 1855, and end on September 16.

2. Of the original journal's fifty-five pages, the first thirty, which cover the journey from August 4 to the 28th, are in pencil and, sadly, so faded they cannot be deciphered. The original journal — a three-by-five-inch notebook — is in a family collection owned by Ellen Holliday, Mt. Kisco, New York.

3. Halliday journal, August 29. I own a small encyclopedia with a chapter on navigation that John Halliday carried with him from England. See Rev. David Blair, *The Universal Preceptor or General Grammar* (London: Sir R. Phillips and Company, 1828).

4. Grosse Isle, or Quarantine Island, lies forty-six kilometers upstream from Quebec. Beginning in 1832, the deserted island became a quarantine station for English and Irish immigrants. Between 1832 and 1937, 51,146 immigrants passed through Grosse Isle. In 1837, a typhus epidemic swept through 221 Irish ships, resulting in the deaths of 8,000 people at sea and another 4,500 whose corpses were removed when the ships reached shore. Since 1947, Grosse Isle has been used as a station for secret bacteriological research ("Grosse Isle," *The Canadian Encyclopedia*, 1985 ed.). While the Hallidays were detained at Grosse Isle, John recorded the following monument inscription in his journal: "In this secluded spot lie the mortal remains of 5424 persons who flying from pestilence and famine in Ireland in the year 1847 found in America but a grave."

5. The journal provides further insight into the problems of emigrants who found themselves at the mercy of officialdom: "After all our providing before leaving home it has cost us a sovereign on board ship and here [Grosse Isle] and not done yet. Government take great credit to themselves for the protection they give passengers. But if worse used before the law was enacted than now there case must have been a pitiful one" (September 15). According to one scholar, Canadian ports "were among the dirtiest in the world, full of disease and pestilence. Public facilities were nonexistent in the colonial cities; open ditches of sewage and filth were common; public houses and hotels overcrowded with immigrants, ignored hygiene precautions" (Audrey Y. Morris, *Gentle Pioneers: Five Nineteenth-Century Canadians* [Toronto: Hodder and Stoughton, 1968], 37).

6. This quotation is taken from the final page of the original journal. The published version of John Halliday's journal follows the original with very few omissions. The

journal ends midsentence on September 16, 1855. Although I imagine that John kept a journal most of his life, only this one survives.

5. My Journey to Checkerberry Village, Vermont

1. Sarah Stannard's birthplace is marked by a granite monument commemorating her brother, Gen. George J. Stannard.

Sarah's grandfather Samuel Stannard was born in Killingworth, Connecticut, in 1749. As a soldier in the American Revolution, he made shoes, moccasins, and snow packs for Washington's army at Valley Forge. Around 1780, Samuel moved to Georgia, Vermont, where his son Samuel was born in 1786. The younger Samuel and his wife, Rebecca Pattee, had thirteen children between 1806 and 1825. Their ninth child, Sarah, married Jason Brown in 1841, and their son Warrington was born June 4, 1845.

Sources for Brown-Stannard genealogy were compiled from genealogical records, Chittenden County Historical Society, Milton, Vermont, and records kept by my aunt Anne, who copied the Brown genealogy from Jason and Sarah Brown's Bible.

2. These names are recorded in the Brown family Bible. The children were born in the following years: Eliza, 1848; Alma, 1850; twins Losey and Lelila (the Bible says "Leila"), 1852.

3. Ivan Sanderson, personal interview, June 21, 1984.

4. Chittenden County, Vermont, map (New York: H. F. Walling Company, 1857).

5. Other sites related to the life of General Stannard are located north of Milton near Georgia Center. In 1907, the state of Vermont and Georgia township raised $1,400 to erect a monument near the site of Stannard's birthplace. Situated on a hill overlooking Lake Champlain, this impressive marker, enclosed by an ornate iron fence, stands in a farm field. When the monument was dedicated in 1908, Stannard's birthplace stood on the east side of the highway that runs in front of the monument. This was the Samuel Stannard log house that my grandfather visited in 1924. Neither house nor farm exists today.

6. The Wisconsin Experience and the Landscape of War

1. Sources relating to the Brown family during their years in Wisconsin are found in the genealogical record copied by Anne Brown Winters from the now missing Jason and Sarah Brown family Bible, the 1875 Minnesota census, and Arthur P. Rose, *An Illustrated History of the Counties of Rock and Pipestone, Minnesota* (Luverne, Minn.: Northern History Publishing Company, 1911).

2. A portrait of Sarah Stannard Brown, once in the author's possession, is now missing. My aunt told me the story of the injured finger when I was a child.

3. Adjutant General, *The Regimental Descriptive Rolls, 1861, 1865, Second Infantry and Independent Battalion*, Wisconsin National Guard. Bound copies of the original handwritten company rosters (from which my data are taken) and a reprinted set, *Wisconsin Vol-*

unteers, War of the Rebellion, 1861–1865 (Madison: Democrat Printing Co., 1914), are housed in the Wisconsin Historical Society, Madison.

4. My search for references to my ancestors in Rock County warranty deeds, assessor's records, plat maps, and census records turned up few leads. The single Halliday citation appears in the 1860 federal census. Jason Brown's enlistment record cites Center as his place of residence. The 1861 Rock County plat map includes one "Brown" near Center in section 24. Although a Jason and a Sarah Brown appear in the *Rock County Gazetteer, Directory, and Business Advertiser, 1857–8*, in the Janesville Public Library, these names do not reappear in later editions.

5. Out of eighty-three privates recorded in the roster of Company D, Second Regiment, Wisconsin Volunteers (*Regimental Descriptive Rolls*, Wisconsin Historical Society), Jason Brown was one of the five enlistees over the age of forty. The *Company Muster-in Roll*, Veterans' Records, National Archives and Records Service, Washington, D.C., states that Jason was a farmer. I have been unable to determine whether or not Jason owned land, rented land, or worked for another farmer.

6. Alan T. Nolan, *The Iron Brigade: A Military History* (New York: Macmillan, 1961), 4–7. According to Nolan, men who enlisted before May 16, 1861, signed up for a three-month term. On the same day, the term of service was changed to three *years*. Because his regimental roll shows he enlisted two days after the change, Jason must have known that he had signed up for the longer period.

7. Ibid., 8–9.

8. William C. Davis, *Battle at Bull Run: A History of the First Major Campaign of the Civil War* (Garden City: Doubleday, 1977), 204–5. The Henry Hill marker states that Judith Henry was killed by artillery fire directed at Confederate sharpshooters in the house. I visited the Bull Run battlefield on June 2–3, 1984, and July 4–5, 1991. Park rangers Michel Andrews, J. W. Burgess, Alan Libby, and Georgia Moss helped me find records and interpret events related to the Wisconsin Second.

9. John Hennessey, *The First Battle of Manassas: An End to Innocence, July 18–21, 1861* (Lynchburg: Privately printed, 1989), 102–3.

10. Ibid., 103.

11. Alan Libby, personal interview, July 5, 1991. The Wisconsin Second lost twenty-three killed, sixty-five wounded, and sixty-three taken prisoner (Nolan, *The Iron Brigade*, 9).

12. The Wisconsin Second *Company Muster-in Roll*, August 31, 1861, records that Jason was "missing since battle of 21 July. Supposed to have been killed on the field." The *Muster-out Roll*, June 29, 1864, notes that Jason was killed in action (Veterans' Records, National Archives and Records Service, Washington, D.C.). Most of the casualties, Libby told me, were sent home or buried in unmarked graves. According to my aunt Anne, Jason was buried on the battlefield (Anne Winters, letter to Warrington Winters, April 15, 1961).

13. An "Amanda Skelley Scrapbook" is housed in the Rock County Historical Society, Janesville. The scrapbook contains obituaries of Sarah Brown and Loammi and Almira Stannard. Sarah Brown's obituary identifies her surviving children in 1896: Warrington and Lucas; Mrs. W. A. (Nettie) Carpenter, Milwaukee; Mrs. Thomas

(Sarah) Schutte and Myra (Almina) M. Brown, Appleton; and Mrs. Joshua (Charlotte) Crall, Janesville. I have been unable to identify Amanda Skelley.

7. The Stannards of Taylors Falls, Minnesota

1. The Stannard branch enters my family tree through my great-grandmother Sarah Stannard, Warrington Brown's mother. Samuel and his wife, Jemima (Wilcox) Stannard, had five children: Betsey, Daniel, Charlotte, Heman, and Samuel, Jr. Samuel, Jr., a prosperous merchant, farmer, and veteran of the War of 1812, married Rebecca Pattee. Of their children, four — Sarah, Loammi, George Jerrison, and Lucas — appear in my narrative (Stannard Papers, author's file).

2. Jeremiah Clemens and J. Fletcher Williams, *United States Biographical Dictionary and Portrait Gallery of Eminent and Self-Made Men*, Minnesota volume (New York: American Biographical Publishing Company, 1879), 456. In 1838, Jesse Taylor staked his claim on land that became Taylors Falls. Taylor and B. F. Baker erected a mill and built a dam and a blacksmith shop in 1839. The town was named in Taylor's honor in 1851 (J. Fletcher Williams, *History of Washington County and the St. Croix Valley* [Minneapolis: North Star Printing Co., 1881], 304).

3. "Stannard, Last of the Constitution Makers of '57 Dies at Taylor [*sic*] Falls," *Minneapolis Journal*, February 2, 1914, and Stannard obituary, *Taylors Falls Standard-Press*, February 5, 1914.

4. Williams, *History*, 308. The careers of Folsom and Stannard run in parallel lines. In 1836, Folsom, nineteen, arrived in Wisconsin Territory, where he worked at odd jobs to earn money to enter business. After forming the Stillwater Boom Company, Folsom and his partners made loggers' rafts for fifty-eight years. Folsom arrived in Taylors Falls in 1850, where along with Stannard he served in the 1857 Constitutional Convention. Folsom's *Fifty Years in the Northwest* (St. Paul: Pioneer Press, 1888) is an excellent source for the study of pioneer life in Minnesota. Folsom's elegant home on Angel Hill is an architectural landmark.

5. E. V. Smalley, *A History of the Republican Party* (St. Paul: E. V. Smalley, 1896), 288–89.

6. Ibid., 259; Clemens and Williams, *United States Biographical Dictionary*, 457.

7. Smalley, *A History*, 289.

8. Stannard obituary.

9. Bonnie Lundberg Clayton, phone interview, June 22, 1994.

10. Kaye Grossmann, personal interview, August 13, 1985.

11. Ibid.

12. *Chisago County News*, September 24, 1891.

13. Grossmann interview.

14. Luke Stannard obituary, *St. Croix Falls Standard-Press*, April 13, 1949. In 1891, Luke married Lottie Sly of Birmingham, Michigan, who in the late 1880s had joined relatives in Taylors Falls, where she became a teacher. The Stannards had three children: Luella, Louise, and Conway ("Wedding Bells," *Chisago County News*, Taylors

Falls, October 15, 1891, and Lottie (Sly) Stannard obituary, *St. Croix Falls Standard-Press*, September 18, 1943). Luke studied at Carleton during the fall semester of 1878 and fall and winter semesters, 1879 (Eric Hillemann, college archivist, phone interview, June 12, 1996).

15. Grossmann interview.

16. Kaye Grossmann, personal interviews, August 13, 1985, and July 14, 1990. Ms. Grossmann gathered stories about the Stannard family at the time Ruth and Conway Stannard revisited the farm in 1978. Ruth told Ms. Grossmann that Luke was a "poor manager," which suggests that the Depression was not the only factor leading to the bank's collapse. At the time of my first visit, Ms. Grossmann phoned Conway, who lived in Ohio, to confirm these family stories. I regret that I failed to contact Conway Stannard, who died soon after my visit. In 1985, I visited Louise Stannard Lundberg, eighty-nine, who was then living in a St. Croix Falls nursing home. According to Mrs. Lundberg, Luke eventually paid back all his creditors. Other stories were told to me by Louise's daughter Bonnie Lundberg Clayton, phone interview, June 22, 1984, and by Conway's daughter-in-law Jean Stannard, phone interview, June 23, 1994.

17. "Luke Stannard to Note 80th Anniversary at Family Home," *Taylors Falls Journal*, June 22, 1939.

8. The Hallidays, Hollidays, and Browns of Goodhue County, Minnesota

1. Quoted in Peg Meier, *Bring Warm Clothes: Letters and Photographs from Minnesota's Past* (Minneapolis: *Minneapolis Tribune*, 1981), 6.

2. My information comes from census records, maps, atlases, land deeds, and many on-site visits. Hazel Wimmer and William Witt were most cooperative in helping me to understand the farm sites and explain recent changes that have taken place on the ridge. Other helpful sources include Alfred T. Andreas, *Illustrated Historical Atlas of the State of Minnesota* (Chicago: A. T. Andreas, 1874); Rose, *An Illustrated History*; U.S. census records, 1860 and 1870; and the 1875 Minnesota census.

3. Throughout this study I have retained the *a* in Halliday as the spelling used by John and Anne Halliday. John Halliday's three sons and their descendants spell their name with an *o*. William's granddaughter told me that "before coming to America your great-grandfather's name was spelled *Halliday* with an 'a' instead of an 'o' but on arriving here when giving his name, with his strong Scotch accent, it was invariably written down as *Holliday*, so he accepted it as such" (Florence Jean Holliday Foster, letter to the author, June 15, 1991).

4. Florence Jean Foster describes her grandmother's death as follows: "the hardship, the isolation, and the privations became too much for [Martha], and after three years [she died and] her body was buried in a plot of ground on one of the beautiful bluffs south of [Red Wing]" (ibid.). Accounts of the life of Joseph Woods Hancock are found in J. W. Hancock, *Goodhue County, Minnesota, Past and Present* (Red Wing: Red Wing Printing Company, 1893) and Madeline Angell and Mary C. Miller, *Joseph Woods Hancock: The Life and Times of a Minnesota Pioneer* (Minneapolis: Dillon Press, 1980). Ex-

cerpts from Hancock's unpublished diary are found in the Angell and Miller study. Ellen Holliday, Mt. Kisco, New York, owns the original copy of Joseph Hancock's diary.

5. Angell and Miller, *Joseph Woods Hancock,* 186.

6. Ibid., 184, 186; Hancock, *Goodhue County,* 444. By the 1870s, Goodhue County's Anglo-American settlers had begun moving west in search of new land. The following immigration wave brought German Lutheran settlers, who in 1881 built a new building on the Presbyterian church site. The congregation of the West Florence Immanuel Lutheran Church remains active there today.

7. William and Dora Witt, personal interviews, June 16, 1983. I spent a wonderful afternoon with the Witts poring over books and papers related to the history of Florence township.

8. A majority of my fieldwork at the William and Marilla Holliday farm was carried out over a two-day period in June 1983. During several trips back throughout the 1980s, I saw that the ruined farm site had remained unchanged. Why this once elegant farm was allowed to fall into ruin is beyond my comprehension.

9. Morris, *The Inhabitants,* n.p.

10. Tom Meersman, "Nuclear Storage Sites Too Close for Comfort," *Minneapolis Star-Tribune,* April 30, 1995.

9. The Browns of Pipestone County, Minnesota

1. George M. Schwartz and George A. Thiel, *Minnesota's Rocks and Waters: A Geological Story* (Minneapolis: University of Minnesota Press, 1954, 1963), 284. The Coteau begins as a continuation of the Drift Prairie in North Dakota and extends south past Lake Traverse and Big Stone Lake and between the James and Minnesota Rivers to the Blue Earth River in northern Iowa. On William Clark's 1810 map, the approximate area is labeled "High Land covered with Wood called Mountain of the Prairie" (Charles O. Paullin, ed., *Atlas of the Historical Geography of the United States* [Washington, D.C.: Carnegie Institute, 1932], plate 32). The term Coteau des Prairies was used by William H. Keating, the geologist who accompanied Stephen Long's expedition in 1823 (Edmund C. Bray and Martha Coleman Bray, *Joseph M. Nicollet on the Plains and Prairies* [St. Paul: Minnesota Historical Society, 1976], 21).

2. Quoted in Rose, *An Illustrated History,* 253.

3. Brian W. Dippie, *Catlin and His Contemporaries: The Politics of Patronage* (Lincoln: University of Nebraska Press, 1990), 42. The quarry's beauty and its history further enhance the romance surrounding the Coteau. The quarry site contains a western-facing wall of Sioux quartzite (jasper), thirty feet in elevation, running north and south. Beneath this massive wall of hard stone and several feet below ground level lies a thinly bedded, fifteen-inch-thick layer of softer stone called pipestone or catlinite. Contemporary Native American craftspeople quarry and sculpt this stone to this day.

4. Rena Neumann Coen, *Painting and Sculpture in Minnesota 1820–1914* (Minneapolis: University of Minnesota Press, 1976), 6. Catlin's painting of the quarry, *Pipestone*

Quarry, on the Coteau des Prairies, 1836–1837, #337, is reproduced in William H. Truettner, *The Natural Man Observed: A Study of Catlin's Indian Gallery* (Washington, D.C.: Smithsonian Institution Press, 1979), 35. Catlin's painting is a generalized view of the quarry site showing Winnewissa Falls, the quartzite ledge, a group of natives watching a warrior cutting stone, and the giant boulders known as the Three Maidens. Catlin wrote that he "bivouacked on the [quarry's] very ridge where nought on earth is seen in [the] distance save the thousand treeless, bushless, weedless hills of grass and vivid green which all around me vanish into an infinity of blue and azure" (quoted in Dippie, *Catlin,* 43).

5. George Catlin, *Letters and Notes on the Manners, Customs, and Conditions of the North American Indians* (London: David Bogue, 1844), 2:168.

6. Bray and Bray, *Joseph N. Nicollet,* 22. Nicollet's map (originally published in 1842 by the Bureau of the Corps of Topographical Engineers) has been reproduced in book form as *The Hydrographical Basin of the Mississippi River, 1843* (St. Paul: Minnesota Historical Society, 1976). In 1843, Nicollet's map and report appeared in *Senate Documents,* 26th Cong., 2nd sess., 1843, S. Doc. 237. Nicollet's journals have been gathered by Martha Coleman Bray, ed., *The Journals of Joseph N. Nicollet: A Scientist on the Mississippi Headwaters with Notes on Indian Life, 1836–37* (St. Paul: Minnesota Historical Society, 1970).

7. Bray and Bray, *Joseph N. Nicollect,* 22.

8. Ibid., 72–73.

9. Abbie Gardner-Sharp, *History of the Spirit Lake Massacre* (Des Moines: Iowa Printing Company, 1885), 176. Seven years after she published her history, Abbie revisited the quarry (Rose, *An Illustrated History,* 256–57).

10. Rose, *An Illustrated History,* 257–60.

11. Ibid., 262–63.

12. O. E. Rölvaag, *Giants in the Earth* (New York: Harper, 1929), 9.

13. Ibid., 9–10.

14. Ibid., 38.

15. Ibid.

16. Rose, *An Illustrated History,* 268fn.

17. Ibid., 666.

18. Ibid., 675.

19. Warrington B. Brown, personal interview with Ellen Pike, 1926.

20. Rose, *An Illustrated History,* 267.

21. *Pipestone County Star,* October 30, 1879, Newspaper Files, Pipestone County Museum.

22. Ibid., July 10, 1879.

23. Rose, *An Illustrated History,* 282.

24. Ibid., 672.

25. Ibid., 684.

26. Pike interview.

27. The present owner of Grandfather's farm discovered the walls while cutting holes for electrical outlets. Albert Blom, personal interview, July 3, 1983. The base of

the walls can be seen from the cellar. I have studied a similar stone-wall house, built ca. 1890, on a farm in Sweet township (William P. Farmer, Jr., personal interview, October 7, 1987).

10. North Dakota Pioneers

1. Officials in Barnes, Steele, and Kidder Counties, North Dakota, helped me search for deed records, plat maps, atlases, and oral sources related to the Halliday family. John Francis Holliday's granddaughter Dorothy Haltom of Houston, Texas, and I have corresponded since 1987. Viola Stramblad Liessman's son Emerson O. Liessman of Bismarck, North Dakota, kindly lent me invaluable biographical material (cited below) that sheds light on both family life and pioneer society in North Dakota. A copy of Houghton Holliday's memoirs (see note 14) was sent to me by William Holliday's granddaughter Florence Jean Holliday Foster of Mariposa, California. Phone conversations with Mrs. Foster helped me to locate William's great-granddaughter Ellen Holliday of Mt. Kisco, New York, where I had a chance to study papers related to the Halliday/Holliday family.

2. Elwyn B. Robinson, *History of North Dakota* (Lincoln: University of Nebraska Press, 1966), 134.

3. Ibid., 144–45.

4. Theodore C. Blegen, *Minnesota: A History of the State* (Minneapolis: University of Minnesota Press, 1963), 298.

5. Federal Writers Project of the Works Progress Administration, *North Dakota: A Guide to the Northern Prairie State, American Guide Series* (New York: Oxford, 1950), 106.

6. Robinson, *History*, 158.

7. Ibid., 148–49.

8. Federal Writers Project, *North Dakota*, 47.

9. Thomas Elliott, *Barnes County History* (Dallas: Taylor, 1977), 5.

10. Ibid., 6.

11. A. T. Andreas, *Historical Atlas of Dakota* (Chicago: R. R. Donnelley and Sons, 1884).

12. Benson's addition in Sanborn, where the family owned investment lots, and the Alta township site appear on the plat map of Valley City in *Standard Atlas of Barnes County, North Dakota* (Chicago: Alden Publishing Company, 1910), 10–11, 67. My sister and I interviewed Myron Olson, Sanborn, North Dakota, in 1985 and 1987.

13. *1879–1979: 100 Years of Happenings in Sanborn* (Litchfield Bulletin, n.d.), 1; Federal Writers Project, *North Dakota*, 269.

14. Houghton Holliday, "Stories I Tell My Grandchildren," unpublished memoir, Oakhurst, California, 1971, 3–5. Houghton Holliday was born in 1882 in Sanborn, North Dakota. He served on the faculty of the Columbia University School of Dental and Oral Surgery from 1928 to 1954, where he was also an associate dean. Dr. Houghton Holliday obituary, *New York Times*, November 26, 1972, 85.

According to Dr. Holliday's memoir, his father's invention was motivated by the sight of men who had lost their arms in threshing machines. William's humanitarianism is documented by the story of his visit to a Chicago manufacturer of farm implements: "The owner took [William] through the plant. In one poorly lit, dirt floored room some thirty or forty men pumped with one foot grindstones as they put an edge on the plows they were making. The air was so filled with the dust from the grinding that one could scarcely see across the room. [William] remarked, 'This must be pretty hard on the men to work in here.' To which the owner replied, 'There are plenty more men'" (Holliday, "Stories," 5).

15. John Francis Holliday, age six months, Tiffany Post Office, Wisconsin, is recorded in the 1860 Wisconsin census. Holliday's biography appears in *The Fiftieth Anniversary of Tuttle, 1911–1961* (n.p., n.d.), 151–53.

16. "John Francis Holliday and Family" in *The Fiftieth Anniversary*, 151. Historian Edna Waldo notes that families gathered the bones and sold them for six to ten dollars a ton. She wrote, "The prairies were white with them, so ruthless had been the slaughter of the great beasts that had meant food, clothing, and shelter to the Indians" (Edna LaMoore Waldo, *Dakota: An Informal Study of the Indians* [Caldwell: Caxton Printers, 1936], 335).

17. "John Francis Holliday and Family," in *The Fiftieth Anniversary*, 152.

18. Ted Haibeck, personal interview, Bostonia, North Dakota, June 1987. The Haibecks own the Bostonia site.

19. "J. F. Holliday," in *Diamond Jubilee, 1881–1956, Steele, N. Dak.* (Mandan: Crescent Printing Company, n.d.), 215.

20. "John Francis Holliday and Family," in *The Fiftieth Anniversary*, 152.

21. Viola Stramblad Liessman, "North Kidder County, North Dakota," in *Diamond Jubilee*, 19–23 (hereafter cited in text), and "Charles Liessman," in ibid., 178–80.

22. Marilla Holliday, "Fifteen Months on a North Dakota Claim," unpublished memoir, Holliday family papers, Mt. Kisco, New York, 1. An edited version appears in appendix 4.

23. Ellen Holliday, phone interview, December 18, 1993.

11. My Journey to Glencolumbkille, Ireland

1. "Funeral of the Late Mrs. J. H. Morgan," *Pipestone County Star*, March 18, 1917. Joseph Homer Morgan died August 23, 1912.

2. *Glencolmcille Failte Welcome* (Ballyshannon: *Donegal Democrat*, n.d.).

3. Aidan Manning, *Glencolumbkille, 3000 B.C.–1885 A.D.* (Ballyshannon: *Donegal Democrat*, 1985), 1–4.

4. Ibid., 92.

5. Ibid., 74.

6. Ibid.

12. My Father's Story

1. The American branch of the Morgan family to which I belong stems from three brothers, James, John, and Miles, sons of William and Elizabeth (Winter) Morgan of County Brecon, Wales. James migrated to Connecticut, John to Virginia, Miles to Springfield, Massachusetts. Miles's son David married Mary Clark. Their son Deacon David married Deborah Colton and moved from Springfield to Brimfield, Massachusetts. David's son Joseph, a sergeant in King George's War, married Margaret Cooley. Joseph, Jr., married Sarah Mighell, and their son Nathaniel married Polly Wheeler. A son, William Towner Morgan, born in Adams, Massachusetts, married Minerva H. Stevens. Their son, my grandfather Joseph Homer Morgan, was born in Henderson, New York ("Morgan Genealogy," author's private papers).

2. Deed records show that Joseph Morgan purchased a portion of section 9, Sherman township, in October 1870. George Barnard, a settler who arrived a year before Joseph Morgan, found only eleven families living in the township. That spring, Bernard had to unload his wagon four times in one day because deep mud hampered travel over the undeveloped roads ("Reminiscences of Story County, Iowa," Iowa Room, Grinnell College Library, Grinnell, Iowa).

3. According to his obituary, Joseph Morgan settled on a farm belonging to J. H. Nichols in Sweet township (Joseph Homer Morgan obituary, *Pipestone County Star*, August 23, 1912).

4. Homer Martens, personal interviews, December 1, 1987, August 27, 1988.

5. Courtenay Morgan-Forman, "Things I Remember about My Father, W. T. (Will) Morgan," unpublished memoir, January 2, 1971, 2. Will married Mabelle Courtenay Brown in 1910, and the couple had five children between 1911 and 1933.

6. Alan Morgan, "Memories of Dad," unpublished essay, April 2, 1972, 7–8.

7. "Pipestone High School To-Day," in *The Pipestone High School Annual, '05* (Pipestone: Star Printing Company, 1905), 15–16. Mother took a year of Latin grammar followed by a year each of Caesar, Cicero, and Virgil. She often said her education provided her with a lifetime of things to think about while washing dishes.

8. Morgan, "Memories of Dad," 11.

9. Sam Hirschy, "Football," in *The Pipestone High School Annual, '05*, 38–39. In 1902, Pipestone outscored its opponents 129 to 15 to share the state championship with Blue Earth, Minnesota. In its seven-game season in 1903, Pipestone scored 119 to 12. In 1904, with many players ineligible because of low academic scores, the team outscored opponents 206 to 0. These teams were coached by Warrington Brown, Will Morgan's future brother-in-law. Stan Morgan tape-recorded articles about Pipestone's undefeated teams as they appeared in southwestern Minnesota newspapers (Stan Morgan, "Pipestone Football, 1902–1903," oral tape, William T. Morgan papers).

10. In 1905, Frank Gotch, an Iowa farmboy, defeated Tom Jenkins, a national wrestling hero, whose reputation matched that of the boxer John L. Sullivan. Gotch went on to defeat George Hackenschmidt, the world champion, in 1908 and 1911. Farmer Burns, Gotch's trainer at Washington High School, Cedar Rapids, Iowa,

fought in over six thousand matches and was largely responsible for making wrestling a structured high school sport (Mike Chapman, *Encyclopedia of American Wrestling* [Champaign: Leisure Press, 1990], 1–2). Burns and Gotch were role models for young boys all over the Midwest. Pipestone's local wrestling hero, Ralph A. Prunty, was an alternate in the 1928 Olympics in Amsterdam (ibid., 24).

11. Morgan, "Memories of Dad," 24.

12. Loran Brown Morgan, letter to the author, November 20, 1993.

13. Although Grandfather tried to shelter his daughters (Aunt Ruth, a nurse and the family rebel, was an exception), he encouraged his sons to pursue careers. Uncle Paul became a prominent surgeon, Garfield a corporate attorney, and Warrington a police officer and sheriff.

Prior to 1900, women were not allowed to enroll in the College of Agriculture. In the late nineteenth century, Minnesota legislators challenged the idea of teaching household arts at the university: "'Girls could best learn by helping their mothers,' [legislators said]. The extra expense of educating women also worried them, and they lamented the 'responsibility of maintaining good moral standards with a student population consisting of both sexes'" (Deidre Nagy, "Research Results for the Home," *Minnesota Science* [Spring 1975]: 25). Ironically, Warrington Brown, whose own education ended in the third grade, served in the Minnesota legislature during the late 1880s.

14. Courtenay Morgan-Forman, "Courtenay — History," unpublished memoir, May 1993.

15. Morgan-Forman, "Things I Remember," 1.

16. Ibid.

17. Alan Morgan, letter to the author, November 11, 1993.

18. Stan Morgan, personal interview, November 23, 1993.

19. Morgan, "Memories of Dad," 10.

20. Stan Morgan, letter to the author, November 18, 1993.

21. When I was a boy, Stan took me and his sons Robert and Stephen on yearly trips to Leech Lake. In September 1985, Stan, Loran, and I spent several days at Leech Lake, where we shared family stories. These journeys are among my best memories.

22. Courtenay Morgan-Forman, "Things I Remember," 2.

23. Stan Morgan, personal interview, November 23, 1993.

24. Loran Morgan, letter to the author, August 3, 1992.

25. Rev. Evert L. Jones, "He Was a Good Man," unpublished funeral oration, First Presbyterian Church, Pipestone, Minnesota, January 16, 1933.

Appendix 2. The Architecture of a Craftsman Bungalow

1. Mervin Vern Palmer was born in Cerro Gordo County, Iowa, in 1878, and moved in 1905 to Flandreau, South Dakota, where he first practiced the building trade as a carpenter and later as a contractor. Palmer built many commercial buildings and homes, including his own residence at 505 Pipestone Avenue East, Flandreau, a structure that strongly resembles our house ("Rites Conducted Friday Afternoon

for M. V. Palmer," *Moody County Enterprise*, Flandreau, South Dakota, September 14, 1961).

2. "Pipestone, Minn., the City of Improvements," *Pipestone Leader*, July 10, 1919. The rediscovery of the bungalow by architectural historians in recent years has produced a search for definitions. Alan Gowans argues that the definition of the true bungalow form should fulfill three of the four features found in the original ca. 1880 Bengalese indigo plantation bangala house: (1) the absence of a basement, (2) a broad expanse of roof, (3) a one-, one-and-a-half-, or two-story house if that story is "disguised by some device such as a roofline breaking through," and (4) the interpenetration of inner and outer space (Alan Gowans, *The Comfortable House: North American Suburban Architecture, 1890–1930* [Cambridge: MIT Press, 1987], 76–77). Omitting feature one, the Morgan house meets Gowans's definition.

Schweitzer and Davis argue that the larger two-story bungalow should be labeled "Craftsman." In its first (1914) catalog, the Lewis Manufacturing Company calls a two- or two-and-one-half-story Craftsman house a "semi-bungalow" (Robert Schweitzer and Michael W. R. Davis, *America's Favorite Homes: Mail-Order Catalogues as a Guide to Popular Early 20th-Century Houses* [Detroit: Wayne State University Press, 1990], 152).

3. Although Sears, Roebuck was not the only company to produce mail-order prefabricated houses, it was the largest and, presently, the best documented. Between 1908 and 1940, Sears produced some 450 designs and shipped approximately 100,000 individual structures. Filling two freight cars, a disassembled house would be shipped to the purchaser along with a seventy-five-page construction manual and blueprints showing elevations, floor plans, and framing details. Sears's Honor-Bilt line guaranteed high-quality structural framing, sheathing, interior trim, flooring, and siding (Katherine Cole Stevenson and H. Ward Jandl, *Houses by Mail: A Guide to Houses from Sears, Roebuck and Company* [Washington, D.C.: Preservation Press, 1986], 19, 29–30).

A major difference between our house and the Sears house is cost. Sears provided a complete package of precut materials for its homes, including "millwork, cabinetry, lath, roofing materials, flooring, siding, building paper, downspouts, doors, window sash, shutters . . . nails, paint, and varnish." Optional material included cement, brick, plaster, screens, storm windows, plasterboard and plumbing, heating and electrical fixtures (ibid., 29). Even considering the added costs of a lot, a foundation, builder's fee, and labor, there is a large difference in cost between "The Westly" ($1,874) and my parents' house ($12,000).

4. When my brothers were at home, all "storms" and screens were changed twice a year. The task of changing windows on the second story was extremely dangerous. I cannot remember a time when all the storms or screens were on during the appropriate seasons.

Appendix 3. Gen. George J. Stannard, Forgotten Hero of the Civil War

1. Sherman R. Moulton, "George Jerrison Stannard," in *Vermonters*, ed. Walter H. Crockett (Brattleboro: Stephen Daye Press, 1931), 202.

2. The secretary of war called for one infantry regiment from Vermont numbering 750. As colonel of the Fourth Militia Regiment, Stannard notified Vermont's adjutant general that he could muster 200 men "to march at twelve hours notice" (G. G. Benedict, *Vermont in the Civil War: A History of the Part Taken by the Vermont Soldiers and Sailors in the War for the Union, 1861–5* [Burlington: Free Press Association, 1886], 1:18). According to Benedict, Stannard was the first Vermonter to volunteer his services.

3. Col. Albert Clarke, "Honors to Stannard," speech given at the dedication of the Stannard Monument, Georgia, Vermont, as printed in the *St. Albans Daily Messenger*, October 12, 1909, 3. Clarke, who served with Stannard at Gettysburg, left a comprehensive account of the general's career in his dedication speech.

4. Ibid., 3.

5. This anecdote is recounted in Richard Wheeler, *Lee's Terrible Swift Sword* (New York: HarperCollins, 1992), 85–86.

6. Tony L. Trimble, "Paper Collars: Stannard's Brigade at Gettysburg," *Gettysburg Magazine* (January 1990): 75.

7. Clarke, "Honors," 4.

8. Champ Clark, *The Civil War: Gettysburg, the Confederate High Tide* (Alexandria: Time-Life Books, 1985), 138–39. When the battle ended, both Stannard and General Winfield Scott Hancock, commander of the Federal II Corps, claimed the honor of ordering the successful flanking maneuver. According to George R. Stewart, "From his moment of first seeing the move of Kemper's brigade to the left, Hancock had decided to throw the Vermonters upon Pickett's flank. Stannard, himself, had the same idea, and by the time that Hancock spurred up, shouting orders, Stannard already had his men in motion" (George R. Stewart, *Pickett's Charge: A Microhistory of the Final Attack at Gettysburg, July 3, 1863* [Boston: Houghton Mifflin, 1959], 231–32). Hancock was standing next to Stannard when a minié ball pierced Hancock's groin, carrying with it a bent ten-penny nail from his saddle. Although severely wounded, Hancock continued to observe the battle after his wound was treated.

9. Stewart, *Pickett's Charge*, 62.

10. Shelby Foote, *The Civil War: A Narrative, Fredericksburg to Meridian* (New York: Random House, 1963), 561.

11. Clarke, "Honors," 5.

12. Benedict, *Vermont*, 465.

13. Clarke, "Honors," 6.

14. Ibid. Clarke noted that Grant himself rode into the fort and personally congratulated Stannard. In his *Memoirs*, Grant wrote: "In one of these assaults upon us, General Stannard, a gallant officer, who was defending Fort Harrison, lost an arm" (Ulysses S. Grant, *Memoirs* [New York: Library of America, 1990], 626).

15. William C. Davis, *Death in the Trenches: Grant at Petersburg* (Alexandria: Time-Life Books, 1986), 142–43. The capture of Fort Harrison is described in detail in Richard J. Sommers, *Richmond Redeemed: The Siege at Petersburg* (Garden City: Doubleday, 1981), 39–49. Sommers calls Stannard "the ablest citizen soldier Vermont sent to the war" (43).

16. Clarke, "Honors," 6.

17. Ibid.

18. "Declaration for the Increase of an Invalid Pension," U.S. Department of the Interior, Pension Office, File #4873, August 25, 1880.

19. Stewart Sifakis, *Who Was Who in the Civil War* (New York: Facts on File, 1988), 616.

20. Clarke, "Honors," 4.

INDEX

Barnes County, N. Dak., 83–84

Barns, 7, 55–56, 60–61, 67

Basements, fear of, 17, 154 n.8

Battle of Bull Run, 52–54

Bax, Arnold, 100

Bennett, Charles H., 75–76

Blain family, Ire., 100

Brennan, Norma, 20

Brown, Amos, 43–47

Brown, Garfield, 3

Brown, George, 46

Brown, Hugh A., 1

Brown, Jason, 42, 50–54

Brown, Lucas (Luke), 64, 76

Brown, Mary Halliday, xiii, 24, 37, 42, 54, 63, 78

Brown, Paul F., 2–3, 78

Brown, Sarah Stannard, 42, 50–54, 57, 64

Brown, Warrington B., xiii, xxi–xxiv, 1–8, 42–44, 52, 64, 67, 76–80

Brown, Warrington S., 3, 7

Brownmoor farm, Scot., 31–35

Burke County, N. Dak., 89–93

Carlyle, Thomas, 29

Carver, Jonathan, 63

Catlin, George, 71–72

Center, Wis., 52, 54–56

Checkerberry Village, Vt., 42–49

Claim shanties, 76, 89–91, 145–147

Clark, Drew, 34–35

Cobble Hill, Colchester County, Vt., 45–49

Collyer brothers, 7, 153–154 n.2

Coteau des Prairie, 70–73

Craftsman architecture, xxi, 11–12, 136–137

Cunningham, Allen, 31

Deetz, James, xxv

De Mag, David, 46–47

Dibble, Roger, 15–16

Dirom family, Scot., 34–35

Donaldson, Ruth, xxii, 7

Ecclefechan, Scot., xxiii, 29–31

Elliott, Thomas P., 83

Fallowfield, David, 28, 31–32

Faugher, Irish townland, 97–100

Field Head (Kilner farm, Cumbria), 22–28

First National Bank, Pipestone, Minn., xxi, 111–112

Folsom, W. H. C., 58

Football, 106–107, 165 n.9

Forman, William F., 106, 137

Fort Mahone, Va., 3

Forum Cafeteria, Minneapolis, 10

Foster, Thomas C., 101

Genaust, Homer, 16–17

Genaust, Jessie, 13

Georgia Center, Vt., 43
Glassie, Henry, xxv
Glencolumbkille, Ire., 94–102
Goodhue County, Minn., 32, 63–68
Grand Central Station, radio show, 17
Great Northern Station, Minneapolis,
 10–12
Great Strickland (Cumbria), xvi
Greek Revival architecture, 45–48, 54–55,
 59–60, 79
Grosse Isle, Quebec, 40–41
Grossmann, Kaye, 59–61

Halliday, Anne Kilner, xiii–xvii, xxii–
 xxiii, 22–28, 36–42, 54, 63–64,
 81–89
Halliday, John, xiii, xxii–xxiv, 7, 29–31,
 36–41, 42, 54, 63–64, 81–89
Halliday, William, 31
Hancock, Joseph Woods, 66
Hancock, Marilla Holliday, 64, 66–67
Harrison family, Cumbria, 23
Heathfield family, Pipestone, Minn., 5–6
Henry, Judith C., 52–53
"Hide the Thimble," 3
Holliday, Ellsworth, 64, 81
Holliday, Francis, 86–87
Holliday, Jenny, 86–87
Holliday, John Francis, 60, 81–89
Holliday, Marilla, 89–93, 143–152
Holliday, Ruth, 86–87
Holliday, William, 37, 39, 42, 54, 66–67,
 81–89
Holm family, N. Dak., 84
Homestead Act of 1862, 82–83

Irving, George and Maybelle, 31

Johnson, Donald, 14

Kidder County, N. Dak., 86–89
Kilner, John, 25
Kilner, William, Jr., 27–28
Kilner, William, Sr., xxii, 25–27

Lake Koronis, Minn., 109–110
Landscapes, xxiv, 22, 30–31, 43–44, 53–
 54, 63–64, 67–68, 69–76, 80, 81, 84,
 94, 100
Last of England, painting, 36–37
Leech Lake, Minn., 111
Let's Pretend, radio show, 17
Liessman, Viola Stramblad, 87–89
Longfellow, Henry W., 74
"Lost fortune" story, 27–28

McDevitt, Colette, 95–97
McGinley, George, 98–100
McGinley, Joe, 98–100
Marshall, Howard Wight, xxv
Martens, Alice, 13
Martens, Homer, 96, 105
Maxwell, Susan, 94–100, 103
Minnesota, natural disasters, 77–78
Morgan, George Alan, 17, 106–108, 110
Morgan, Joseph Homer, 103
Morgan, Loran (Bud), 17, 111–112
Morgan, Mabelle C. Brown, xxi, 1, 8–10,
 11–19, 108–110
Morgan, W. Stannard, 17, 24, 79, 108, 110–
 111
Morgan, Walter, 13, 154 n.4
Morgan, William Towner (father), xxi, 13,
 104–113
Morgan, William Towner, III, 32
Morgan-Forman, Courtenay, xxi, 81–82,
 110–112
Morris, Wright, xxv
Mudcura sanatorium, 18–19

Nelson, Marilyn, 20–21
Nicollet, Joseph N., 71–74
Noren, Catherine Hanf, xxv
Northern States Power Company, 67–68

Our Town, play, 21

Palacios, Tex., 89
Penrith, Eng., 22–23

Pipestone County, Minn., xxiii, 69–80, 104
Pipestone quarry, 72–75

Radi, Donald, 14, 16
Radi, Eddie, 14, 16
Redford, Dorothy, xxv
Rheumatic fever, xiii, xxii, 18, 20
Robinson, Elwyn B., 82
Rolvaag, O. E., 75–76
Rose, Arnold, 76, 78

St. Andrew Church, Penrith, Eng., 30
St. Patrick, immigrant ship, 38–40
Salt lantern, xiii, xvi, 36
Salt lantern house, xvi–xvii, xxiii
Sanborn, N. Dak., 84–85
Sanderson, Ivan, 45, 48
Sharp, Abbie Gardner, 74
Sleepy Eye, Minn., 9–10
Smith, Dorothy, 28
Sod houses, 76, 78
Spirit Lake, Iowa, 74
Stannard, Conway, 61
Stannard, Gen. George J., 44, 48–49,
    138–142
Stannard, Harriet Stevenson, 58–59
Stannard, Loammi K., 50, 54, 60
Stannard, Lottie Sly, 59
Stannard, Lucas K., 57–62
Stannard, Luke, 61–62
Stannard, Rebecca, 43
Stannard, Ruth (Mrs. Conway), 61
Stannard, Samuel, Jr., 43

Stannard, Samuel, Sr., 43
Stannard farm, Taylors Falls, Minn., 59–61
Stannard State Bank, Taylors Falls, Minn.,
    61–62
Stark family, Janesville, Wis., 54–56
Story County, Iowa, 103–104
Stramblad, Theodore, 87–89
Streetcars, 11
Sweet, Daniel, 76

Taylors Falls, Minn., 57–62
Thomson, Janet, 31
Thomson, John, 31–32

Vernacular architecture, 64–67, 105
Victorian architecture, 59–61, 64

Walz, Fred, 13
Wimmer family, Goodhue County, Minn.,
    64
Winters, Anne (Annie) Belle Brown, xiii,
    xxii, 3, 7, 12, 16, 23–24, 27–30, 52, 108,
    131–135
Winters, Donovan, 7
Winters, George W., xiii, xxii, 4–5, 12
Winters, Warrington W., 25, 36
Wisconsin Second Brigade, Bull Run,
    52–54
Witt, William, 66–67
Wolfe, Thomas, 11
World War II: blackouts, 15; gardens,
    15–16; scrap drives, 16
Wrestling, 106, 165 n.10

THE AMERICAN LAND AND LIFE SERIES

Bachelor Bess: The Homesteading Letters
of Elizabeth Corey, 1909–1919
Edited by Philip L. Gerber

Circling Back:
Chronicle of a Texas River Valley
By Joe C. Truett

Edge Effects:
Notes from an Oregon Forest
By Chris Anderson

Exploring the Beloved Country:
Geographic Forays into American Society
and Culture
By Wilbur Zelinsky

Great Lakes Lumber on the Great Plains:
The Laird, Norton Lumber Company in
South Dakota
By John N. Vogel

Hard Places: Reading the Landscape of
America's Historic Mining Districts
By Richard V. Francaviglia

Living in the Depot:
The Two-Story Railroad Station
By H. Roger Grant

Main Street Revisited: Time, Space, and
Image Building in Small-Town America
By Richard V. Francaviglia

Mapping American Culture
*Edited by Wayne Franklin and
Michael C. Steiner*

Mapping the Invisible Landscape:
Folklore, Writing, and the Sense of Place
By Kent C. Ryden

Pilots' Directions: The Transcontinental
Airway and Its History
Edited by William M. Leary

Places of Quiet Beauty: Parks, Preserves,
and Environmentalism
By Rebecca Conard

Reflecting a Prairie Town:
A Year in Peterson
Text and photographs by Drake Hokanson

A Rural Carpenter's World: The Craft in a
Nineteenth-Century New York Township
By Wayne Franklin

Salt Lantern:
Traces of an American Family
By William Towner Morgan